GREAT SHORT STORIES

for

Listening-Speaking

Easy-Reading Adaptations

by David Christiansen

Illustrated by Nori Shirasu

JAG Publications

Published by JAG Publications

11288 Ventura Boulevard

Studio City, California 91604

Telephone & Fax: (818) 505-9002

E-mail: info@jagpublications-esl.com

Web site: www.jagpublications-esl.com

Cover art and illustrations by Nori Shirasu

Production and typesetting by Jack Lanning

Printed in the United States of America

ISBN 0-943327-31-8

First Edition 2005

10 9 8 7 6 5 4 3 2

Table of Contents

How to Use This Book

There are many activities in each lesson. The main part of each lesson is the story, but there are also listening and speaking activities. Each lesson usually takes two days to complete, but it may be longer if the teacher wishes to supplement the lesson.

The information below is one possible outline for the book. After becoming more familiar with the text, the teacher is able to change the format of instruction. There are many ways to use and supplement the textbook. Here is the suggested format:

1. To begin, look at the picture that begins each lesson. As a class, or in small groups, discuss what you think the story will be about according to the picture. You may also have students give their own short stories about the picture as a warm-up speaking activity. **(5-10 minutes)**

2. Play the story. Students may either listen while reading along, or listen with their textbooks closed. Another possible way to use the text is to have one student read the story, then tell the story to a partner. **(10-15 minutes)**

3. Background and Biography: Almost all the authors here are very famous. You will learn a little about them, but you may want to look them up as a special exercise to learn more. Also included is background information for better understanding the story.

4. Review the vocabulary and phrases with the students. Low-intermediate students are encouraged to use their dictionaries as needed. However, much unfamiliar vocabulary can be understood through context. For this reason we would discourage slavish consultation with the dictionary for every unfamiliar word. **(10-15 minutes)**

5. Allow students the chance to write short answers to the questions. Go over the questions about the story as a class or in small groups. **(10-15 minutes)**

6. Proceed with the listening, speaking, and pronunciation exercises. Many of the activities can be done in pairs, small groups, or as a class. For variety, the teacher may wish to switch between pair work, small group work and class work. **(15-45 minutes)**

7. Some of the activities require the teacher to prepare materials in advance, so be sure to look over each lesson before presenting it to the class.

8. The listening activities are labeled with the number of the CD (tape) and the track number. **(Example: Listen: Comprehension (2:15) = CD 2, Track 15)**

Answers to activities in the lessons are provided in the Appendix section of the book.

Lesson 1: The Open Window

Look at the picture below. Discuss what you think the story will be about.

Biography and Background

Saki, the name used by H.H. Munro, (1870-1916), was born in Burma, but lived most of his life in England. He was first a political writer and war correspondent. But later his novels, and especially his short stories made him famous for their mixture of fun and terror. **"The Open Window"** is a good example.

Listen: Comprehension (1:1) Listen to the story.

Option 1: Read along in your book.   **Option 2:** Listen to the story with your book closed.

The Open Window

By Saki (H. H. Munro)

"Please have a seat, Mr. Nuttel. My aunt will be down in a few moments."

Framton Nuttel sat down. He was tired and nervous, and had come to this country house for a week of much needed rest. He looked at the young lady, who was about fifteen, yet seemed very mature and lively for her age. She had an almost mischievous look in her eyes.

"Do you know anyone around here?" the girl asked.

"Not a single person," said Framton. "My sister stayed here four years ago. She gave me some addresses of things to do and see."

"Then you don't know anything about my aunt?" asked the niece.

"Only her name, Mrs. Stapleton, and her address," stated Framton. The question made him wonder about the aunt who had not yet appeared.

"Three years ago she experienced a great tragedy and hasn't been the same since," said the niece. "That would be after your sister was here. Do you see that open window?" She pointed to the large French window leading to the front lawn.

"It's a little cold for the window to be open. But does that window have anything to do with her great tragedy?" asked Framton.

"My aunt keeps the window open, waiting for her husband and two young brothers to return. Three years ago they went out hunting with their dog and never came back. It had been a terribly wet summer, you know, and there were dangerous swamps. No one knows what happened, but their bodies were never found. Poor Aunt, she always keeps the window open, hoping they will come back."

Framton sat there, staring out the window, across the lawn and into the woods.

"Sometimes, on quiet evenings, I get a creepy feeling that they'll all walk in through that window," said the girl.

It was a relief to Framton when the aunt entered the room, apologizing for being late.

"I hope that Vera has been amusing you," she said.

"She has been very interesting," said Framton.

"I hope you don't mind the window open," said Mrs. Stapleton. "My husband and brothers will be home soon from hunting, and they always come in this way. It's rained a lot recently, so they'll make a fine mess over my poor carpets. Sometimes they're so careless."

She continued cheerfully talking on and on about hunting and birds and the lack of ducks in the winter. To Framton it was purely horrible. He tried to change the subject.

"The doctors back home agreed that I should just relax and take it easy," announced Framton. "But they are not so particular about my diet."

"Oh, really?" Mrs. Stapleton seemed quite bored with these details about his health. Suddenly her face brightened. "Here they are at last!" she cried. "Just in time for dinner, and look how muddy they are!"

Framton shivered and looked at the niece. She stared through the window with horror in her eyes. With apprehension turning into fear, he turned in his chair to look in the same direction. Three figures carrying guns, and a dog, walked across the lawn towards the window. Framton grabbed wildly for his hat and coat. He rushed past the two women, out the door, and into the dark afternoon.

"Here we are, my dear," said one of the men, coming in through the window. "Fairly muddy, but most of it's dry. Who was that running out as we came?"

"He was really a strange man. He could only talk about his illness. Then he rushed off without a word of goodbye or apology. He looked like he had seen a ghost."

"I expect it was the dog," said the niece calmly. "He was telling me that he is scared to death of dogs. A couple of years ago in India, he was in a graveyard when a mad dog began attacking him. He fell into an open grave, where the dog stood snarling and barking above him all night. –Enough to make anyone terrified of dogs."

As she told the story, she had a little mischievous look in her eyes.

Vocabulary Find
Read through the story and circle any words or phrases that you don't understand. Discuss the words you circled & the vocabulary below with your teacher, or look them up in a dictionary.

tragedy	mature	lively	mischievous
niece	swamps	creepy	snarling
shivered	horror	apprehension	graveyard

Expressions
Here are related expressions to the topic of the story: **FEAR**. Review as a class.

1. *"You scared me to death."* (You really scared me.)
2. *"It made my skin crawl."* (It made me feel nervous and scared.)
3. *"Don't be such a chicken."* (Don't be so afraid to try new things.)
4. *"I have butterflies in my stomach."* (I am very nervous before performing.)
5. *"Are you a mouse or a man?"* (Are you afraid, or are you brave?)

Writing/Discussion
First, write short answers. Then discuss your answers in groups, or as a class.

1. Who were the main characters in the story? What do we know about them?

   _____

   _____

2. Why was the window left open?

   _____

   _____

3. Why was the ending surprising?

   _____

   _____

4. What do you think happened to Mr. Nuttel?

   _____

   _____

5. How would you have reacted if you were Mr. Nuttel?

   _____

   _____

Let's Talk
In small groups, take turns telling a story about something that happened to you. It may be a true story, or a story that is not true. After hearing a story, group members must decide whether it is true or not true. See if you can fool the group with your story.

Person	Story is True	Story is Not True
1.		
2.		
3		
4.		

Listen: Practice (1:2) Listen to the short stories. Put them in order as you hear them from 1 to 5. Discuss whether you think each story is true or not true and why.

_____ A.   This story is about a group of people who went swimming and almost had an accident.

_____ B.   This story is about a person who lost and found their car keys.

_____ C.   This story is about a person who drove a car from their house to the hospital.

_____ D.   This story is about an old man who survived a boating accident.

_____ E.   This story is about a person who was saved by their dog.

Listen: Vocabulary Fill-in (1:3) First, choose and write the correct word in the sentences below. Then listen to the speakers to check your answers.

1. It was a real _____ when the young boys were hurt in the accident.

   mature   **tragedy**   **lively**   **mischievous**   **creepy**

2. He had a very _____ feeling as he walked inside the old house.

   mature   **tragedy**   **lively**   **mischievous**   **creepy**

3. The little boy was very _____ . He always got into things and made a mess.

   mature   **tragedy**   **lively**   **mischievous**   **creepy**

4. The young woman was very _____ for her age. It was hard to believe she was only 15.

   mature   **tragedy**   **lively**   **mischievous**   **creepy**

5. The party was _____ . Everyone was dancing and playing games and having fun.

   mature   **tragedy**   **lively**   **mischievous**   **creepy**

6. The men walked around in the _____ until their boots were full of mud and water.

   niece   **graveyard**   **swamps**   **shivered**   **apprehension**

7. It was really cold and all the boys _____ as they went outside.

   niece   **graveyard**   **swamps**   **shivered**   **apprehension**

8. The woman's _____ talked to the guests while she was preparing dinner.

   niece   **graveyard**   **swamps**   **shivered**   **apprehension**

Listen: Vowel Sounds (1:4) Repeat after the speakers. Focus on the correct pronunciation.

Short sounds	A	E	I	O	U
	ant	egg	if	on	uncle
Long sounds	A	E	I	O	U
	Late	meet	mine	hole	pool

Repeat each line after the speakers. Focus on the correct pronunciation.

	/ee/	/i/	ay/	/e/	/a/	/o/
1.	beat	bit	bait	bet	bat	bought
2.	lead	lid	laid	led	lad	laud
3.	seal	sill	sale	sell	Sal	Sol
4.	Dean	Din	Dane	den	Dan	Don
5.	read	rid	raid	red	rad	rod
6.	bead	bid	bade	bed	bad	bod
7.	Pete	pit	pate	pet	pat	pot
8.	neat	knit	Nate	net	nat	not

Lesson 2: The Emperor's New Clothes

Look at the picture below. Discuss what you think the story will be about.

Biography and Background

Hans Christian Andersen (1805-1875) was born into a very poor family in Denmark. At age eleven he was sent to work for a weaver and a tailor. He wrote of unfortunate people with great sympathy. Although he wrote novels and plays, he is most remembered for his fairy tales.
"The Emperor's New Clothes" is one of his most famous.

The Emperor's New Clothes

By Hans Christian Andersen

Many years ago there was an Emperor who loved new clothes so much that he spent most of his money on them. One day two strangers entered the town, saying that they knew how to weave the most beautiful clothing imaginable. Not only were the colors and patterns very fine, but the work was of such high quality that it would be invisible to any person who was not loyal to the king.

"These must be wonderful clothes," thought the Emperor. "I will wear them and know who is not loyal to me." He decided to pay the two strangers a large amount of money for the new clothes.

The two men pretended to weave the cloth, but there was nothing in their hands except the tools for making clothes. The emperor sent one of his servants to visit the tailors to see that they were making the new clothes. When the servant arrived, he saw the two men working on what seemed to be clothes, but he could see no material or thread. They asked the servant to come closer to inspect the new clothes. They pointed to the empty places on the table and asked the servant how he liked the clothes.

"Good heavens," thought the servant. "Is it possible that I cannot see the clothing because I am not loyal to the Emperor? I cannot say anything about this." He continued to look wherever the two tailors pointed, hoping to see the clothing.

"So, what do you think?" asked one of them.

"Uh, it is all just beautiful. It's very, very beautiful. I shall tell the Emperor that you are doing a fine job." He returned to the Emperor and reported great things about the new clothes.

Time passed. The Emperor gave the clothes makers more money for more clothes. Then he sent another servant to inspect the clothes. Again the two men pointed to clothes that weren't there, and again there was nothing to be seen.

"I must be disloyal to the Emperor for I cannot see anything!" thought the servant. When the two clothes makers asked his opinion, he replied that they were doing an excellent job. Soon after that, the Emperor himself decided to inspect the new clothes. He had his servants join him to visit the clothes makers.

"It is magnificent!" said the servants. "What a beautiful design, and the colors are absolutely wonderful!"

"What?" thought the Emperor, "I see nothing at all. This is terrible. Does this mean that I am disloyal to my own people? This cannot be." He stared wherever the two clothes makers pointed, but could not see a thing. The Emperor exclaimed,

"These are wonderful. I love the color and design. I shall wear them in tomorrow's parade."

The next day the two tailors asked the Emperor to take off all his clothes. Then they pretended to put new clothes on him. They pretended to fasten something around his waist and to tie things on, but no one could see a thing. Finally the two men stopped and exclaimed,

"Oh, your Majesty! You look so marvelous. The colors and designs are perfect. You've never looked better!" So the Emperor marched out of his castle and paraded around the town. Everyone in the streets shouted compliments about the clothing that they could not see. They did not want to appear disloyal to the Emperor, either. As the Emperor continued his walk about the town, a small boy saw him and exclaimed,

"But he has nothing on!" Soon people began to laugh.

"He has nothing on! He has nothing on!" The Emperor only now knew the truth. The two clothes makers seemed to have disappeared.

Vocabulary Find

Read through the story and circle any words or phrases that you don't understand. Discuss the words you circled & the vocabulary below with your teacher, or look them up in a dictionary.

emperor	patterns	cloth	servant
strangers	invisible	material	parade
weave	loyal	thread	fasten

Expressions
Here are related expressions to the topic of the story: **FOOLISH**. Review as a class.

1. *"A fool and his money are soon parted."* (A foolish person will waste money.)
2. *"Sometimes he is so dense."* (Sometimes he does foolish things.)
3. *"Use your head!"* (Think before doing something.)
4. *"Wake up!"* (Think before doing something.)
5. *"I'm not letting her play me for the fool."* (I'm not going to let her fool me.)

Writing/Discussion
First, write short answers. Then discuss your answers in groups, or as a class.

1. Who were the main characters in the story? What do we know about them?

   _____

   _____

2. What were the two clothes makers doing all day long?

   _____

   _____

3. What did the servants say to the clothes makers and why?

   _____

   _____

4. Why was the Emperor embarrassed at the end of the story?

   _____

   _____

5. What can be learned from the story?

   _____

   _____

Listen: Practice (1:6)
Listen to the people as they describe embarrassing things that happened to them. Match the person to the embarrassing situation.

1. _____ William
2. _____ Robert
3. _____ Sally
4. _____ James
5. _____ Mary

A. person spilled coffee all over his/her clothes in a restaurant
B. person locked his/her keys in his car
C. person forgot his/her professor's name
D. person accidentally broke his/her neighbor's window
E. person gets embarrassed when he/she is asked to sing in public

Let's Talk

In small groups, or as a class, discuss what you would do in the following situations:

1. You thought the movie started at 7:30, but when you walk into the theater, you see it has already started. You can't see your friends anywhere because it is really dark.
2. You see an old friend of yours from school and say hello, but your friend looks at you and doesn't seem to recognize you.

3. Your boss at work gave you an important task to do, but you forgot what it was. You know it must be done before the end of the day, and your boss is in important meetings all day.

4. You are playing games in your yard when suddenly the ball accidentally goes through your neighbor's window.

5 You are eating in a very nice restaurant and you accidentally spill your soup all over the table and yourself. Nobody in the restaurant notices.

6. Some people sitting next to you are talking in the library. Someone comes over and tells all of you to be quiet. You were not the one talking.

Listen: Practice (1:7) Now listen to the six situations from the previous page and write down what the person does in each situation.

Situation	What the Person Would Do
1	
2	
3	
4	
5	
6	

Vocabulary Match Work with a partner. Match the vocabulary words with the correct definition.

emperor   people who nobody knows

strangers   not able to be seen

invisible   the ruler of an empire (larger than a kingdom)

material   someone who is hired to help or serve another person

servant   to attach or make something tight, like a belt

parade   cloth used to make clothing

fasten   march up and down the street for people to see

Listen: The Schwa Sound (1:8) Repeat the words and phrases below after the speakers.

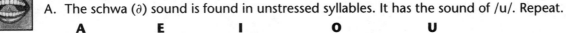

Focus on using the correct pronunciation.

A. The schwa (∂) sound is found in unstressed syllables. It has the sound of /u/. Repeat.

A	**E**	**I**	**O**	**U**
a bout	pro **blem**	cou **sin**	**to** day	cir **cus**

B. The schwa(∂) sound is used for articles (a, an). It has the sound of /u/. Repeat.

A boy and **a** girl.   He ate **an** ice cream cone.   He's **a** good friend.   Wait **an** hour.

C. The schwa (∂) sound is used for prepositions. It has the sound of /u/. Repeat.

She has **to** leave.   A glass **of** water.   He's **from** England.   It's **for** me.

Underline all of the schwa sounds that you hear.

1. He decided not to come for another hour.
2. I put the object in my pocket.
3. It will take about an hour.
4. She is a wonderful neighbor.
5. The magazine contains pictures.
6. The women talked today.

Lesson 3: Hearts and Hands

Look at the picture below. Discuss what you think the story will be about.

Biography and Background

O. Henry, the name used by William Sidney Porter (1862-1910) was American. He said that he could always find a good story in everyday real life. Human nature, romance and make-believe were his specialties. His great popularity was for short stories with surprise endings, such as the short story **"Hearts and Hands."**

Listen: Comprehension (1:9) Listen to the story.

Option 1: Read along in your book.   **Option 2:** Listen to the story with your book closed.

Hearts and Hands

By O. Henry

In Denver there were many passengers boarding a train heading east. In one section of the train sat a very pretty young woman dressed in elegant clothes. Among the new passengers were two men, one very handsome and young, and the other older and rough looking. The two men were handcuffed together at the wrists.

As they passed down the aisle, the only seat available was one facing the attractive young woman. The two men sat down. The young woman looked at one of the men, then smiled at the young, attractive man.

"Well, Mr. Easton, don't you recognize your old friends?"

The young man sat up straight at the sound of her voice and for a moment, seemed embarrassed.

"I believe you must be Miss Fairchild," he said with a smile. You'll have to excuse me for not shaking your hand." He held up the handcuff about his right wrist.

The happy look on the girl's face changed to one of confusion and horror. The young man was about to speak, but was interrupted by the rough looking man seated next to him.

"Please excuse me for interrupting, Miss. I see you've met the marshal here. If you ask him to say a good word for me before I go to prison, I know he'd do it, and I'd be very thankful. I've got seven years of prison for stealing."

"Oh!" said the girl, relaxing and smiling again. "So, this is what you are doing out here. A marshal!"

"Yes, ma'am. I saw this opening in the West and decided that it would be an interesting job to have."

"I should say interesting," replied the young lady. "So now you're one of those Western heroes that rides and shoots and gets into all kinds of dangerous situations." The girl looked down at the handcuffs.

"Don't worry about these things," said the older man. "All marshals handcuff themselves to their prisoners to keep them from getting away. This man knows his business."

"Will I see you again, soon?" asked the young lady.

"Not anytime soon. My work takes me all over the West."

"Well, congratulations on your success," stated the young woman. I'm sure that you are a fine, fine marshal."

"I'm sorry to interrupt you, Marshal," said the other man. "I need a drink and I haven't had a smoke all day. Do you think we could go to the smoking room and get a drink?"

Mr. Easton hesitantly smiled. "Well, I can't deny this man some pleasures of life before we lock him away. It was really nice seeing you again."

"And you," replied the woman. "You take care of yourself."

The two men got up, and walked down the aisle to the next train car. The two passengers in a seat nearby had heard most of the conversation. One of them commented, "That marshal's a good man."

"He seemed pretty young to be a marshal," commented the other.

"Young!" exclaimed the first, "Why, didn't you catch on to what he was doing? Were you fooled as well? Did you ever know a marshal to handcuff a prisoner to his right hand?

Vocabulary Find
Read through the story and circle any words or phrases that you don't understand. Discuss the words you circled & the vocabulary below with your teacher, or look them up in a dictionary.

elegant	handcuffed	horror	train car
rough	wrists	interrupted	hesitantly
handsome	aisle	marshal	commented

Expressions
Here are related expressions to the topic of the story: **CRIME/LAW**. Review as a class.

1. *"We're going to put him away for a long time."* (He will go to prison for a long time.)
2. *"Crime doesn't pay."* (Crime does not help the criminal in the end.)
3. *"He was caught shoplifting."* (He was caught stealing store items.)
4. *"Maybe we can cut you a deal."* (Maybe we can help you out.)
5. *"Can you keep your word?"* (Can you keep your promise?)

Writing/Discussion
First, write short answers. Then discuss your answers in groups, or as a class.

1. Who were the main characters in the story? What do we know about them?

_____

_____

2. Why were the two men handcuffed to each other?

_____

_____

3. Why did the passenger say that the marshal was a good man?

_____

_____

4. What didn't the other passenger understand?

_____

_____

5. Why do you think the marshal did what he did?

_____

_____

Listen: Vocabulary Fill-in (1:10)
First, choose and write the correct word in the sentences below. Then listen to the speakers to check your answers.

1. The young woman's dress was _____ and expensive.

   elegant   **rough**   **handsome**   **horror**   **interrupted**

2. The older man _____ the younger man as he was explaining.

   elegant   **rough**   **handsome**   **horror**   **interrupted**

3. His face and hands were _____ looking and his clothes were torn and dirty.

   elegant   **rough**   **handsome**   **horror**   **interrupted**

4. There was _____ in the woman's eyes when she saw that they were handcuffed.

   elegant   **rough**   **handsome**   **horror**   **interrupted**

5. The young man looked very _____ in his new suit.

   elegant   **rough**   **handsome**   **horror**   **interrupted**

6. The two men were _____ at the wrists.

   handcuffed   **wrists**   **aisle**   **marshal**   **train car**

7. The thief was caught by the _____ and sent to prison.

    handcuffed   **wrists**   **aisle**   **marshal**   **train car**

8. All of the passengers were sleeping in the _____ except for the woman.

    handcuffed   **wrists**   **aisle**   **marshal**   **train car**

Let's Talk
Read the situations below. Discuss what you would do with a partner or as a class.

1. You are with friends in a store and one of your friends is shoplifting.
2. You are in a store and you see a stranger shoplifting.
3. You see a man running towards you, and the police are chasing him.
4. A friend wants to borrow a lot of money from you, but won't tell you why.
5. You are sitting on a bench, when someone steals your backpack and starts running.

Listen: Practice (1:11)
Listen to the situations. Place a number under the picture as it is being described.

_____

_____

_____

_____

_____

_____

Listen: The /i/ and /ee/ sounds (1:12)
Repeat after the speaker.

1. mitt	meat	4. ship	sheep	7. lid	lead
2. fit	feet	5. bit	beat	8. sick	seek
3. live	leave	6. chicks	cheeks	9. sit	seat

Circle the word that you hear the speaker say in the sentences below.

1. The old man (bit / beat) the dog with a stick.
2. He wants to buy a (ship / sheep).
3. The doctors said she is going to (live / leave).
4. Look at those pretty (chicks / cheeks).
5. He forgot to bring his (mitt / meat) to the party.

Now take turns with a partner saying the sentences above. Choose a word to complete the sentence.

Lesson 4: How Much Land Does a Man Need?

Look at the picture below. Discuss what you think the story will be about.

Biography and Background

Leo Tolstoy (1828-1910) a Russian nobleman, wrote of great social problems. His best known work is the huge novel, ***War and Peace***. Most of his fiction came from his diaries, in which he tried to understand his own feelings and actions so that he might control them. Greed is the theme of the following story, ***"How Much Land Does a Man Need?"***

Listen: Comprehension (1:13) Listen to the story.

Option 1: Read along in your book.   Option 2: Listen to the story with your book closed.

How Much Land Does a Man Need?

By Leo Tolstoy

Pakhom, the farmer, listened to his wife talking to her sister, visiting from the city. The sister boasted about the advantages of city life, causing Pakhom to boast in turn, "Our one trouble is—so little land. If I only had as much land as I wanted, I shouldn't be afraid of anyone—even of the Devil."

But the Devil was overhearing from behind the stove, and he said to himself, "You and I'll have to fight it out. I'll give you a lot of land."

One evening, a peddler stopped at his house. As they conversed over a cup of tea, the peddler told Pakhom about a distant fertile valley whose people were not very smart, but had all the land a man could want and would sell it for almost nothing to someone they liked.

Pakhom left his wife to care for his home. With his man servant, he made the long journey to the valley. He brought along many gifts, and tea, and wine. After he gave them the presents, he asked about the land.

"Because you have been so kind to us," the head man said, "we will let you have as much land as you want for 1000 rubles. We will give you one day to walk around and mark off the land that you want. If you do not return to the spot where you started by sundown, you lose the money and the land. If you do return to the starting point, all the land that you marked off will be yours."

Pakhom became very excited. He could hardly sleep that night because he was thinking about all the land that he would get in the morning. Just before sunrise, Pakhom fell asleep and had a dream. He seemed to see himself lying on the ground, with someone laughing. The man who was laughing was the head man of the village.

"What are you laughing at?" he asked. Then the man seemed to change into the peddler whom he had met a few weeks ago. But then he changed again, and this time Pakhom saw no man at all, but the Devil, himself, with horns and hoofs, laughing. He saw a figure lying dead on the ground, shirtless and barefoot. Looking closer, Pakhom realized the dead man was himself.

He suddenly woke up from his dream. The sun was just beginning to rise, and Pakhom wanted to start measuring off his land. The leaders from the village came and greeted him. They placed a cap on the ground. "This is where you start. All that you go around shall be yours if you make it back to this cap before the sun goes down."

Pakhom put his 1000 rubles in the cap, then started to measure off the land. All he could see was rich, fertile land all about him. He began walking, and marking the land as he walked. Soon he was so far away from the leaders that he could barely see them. He decided to take a short rest, then begin turning.

He traveled in a straight line for many miles, then turned again, to head back where he started. He could barely see the men standing at the starting point. The sun was now beginning to set. He felt that he had walked enough and that he had plenty of land now. As he walked, he noticed that the sun was setting quickly, and he was still very far from where he started. He began to walk faster. "I will not make it in time, and I shall lose both the land and my 1000 rubles!" exclaimed Pakhom, and he began walking even faster. He removed all the objects that he was carrying, took off his shirt and boots and started to run. The day was still very hot. Pakhom was tired, but he kept on running.

"I'm not going to make it in time," thought Pakhom. Using all of his energy, he continued running in the dry heat. He could now see the people cheering and urging him on. He could even see the cap on the ground with his 1000 rubles. He noticed one of the men pointing at him and laughing, just like the man in his dream.

Pakhom stumbled to the cap just as the sun went down. He collapsed there as the men cheered. "You have marked yourself a wonderful piece of land," said the head man. He went to Pakhom and tried to help him up, but Pakhom did not move. Pakhom's man servant dug a grave and buried him in his own land. It was just enough land to fit him from head to foot.

Vocabulary Find

Read through the story and circle any words or phrases that you don't understand. Discuss the words you circled and the vocabulary below with your teacher, or look them up in a dictionary.

devil	sundown	rubles	stumble
fertile	miles	barefoot	urging
piece of land	mark off	measuring	collapsed

Expressions

Here are related expressions to the topic of the story: **GREED**. Review as a class.

1. *"He would sell his own mother for money."* (He is only interested in money.)
2. *"She appears a bit money-hungry."* (She wants more and more money.)
3. *"They are really living it up, aren't they?"* (They are enjoying spending a lot of money.)
4. *"I think he sold his soul to the devil."* (He did whatever it took to become successful.)
5. *"He is one tough customer."* (He is hard to please, or it's difficult to sell something to him.)

Writing/Discussion

First, write short answers. Then discuss your answers in groups, or as a class.

1. Who were the main characters in the story? What do we know about them?

   _____

   _____

2. Why did Pakhom leave home and search for new land?

   _____

   _____

3. What do you understand about Pakhom's dream?

   _____

   _____

4. What happened to Pakhom in the end and why did it happen?

   _____

   _____

5. Do you think that most people would have done the same thing that Pakhom did?

   _____

   _____

Vocabulary Match

Match the vocabulary word to its definition. Work in pairs or as a class.

fertile	a measurement of 5,280 feet
sundown	without shoes and/or socks
miles	rich with nutrients, usually referring to dirt or soil
barefoot	time in which the sun goes down and night begins
measure	to trip and fall
stumble	to find the length by using some form of numbering
urge	strong desire to do something

Listen: Practice (1:14) Listen to the speakers as they say an amount of money.

Write out the amount.

1. _____
2. _____
3. _____
4. _____
5. _____

6. _____
7. _____
8. _____
9. _____
10. _____

11. _____
12. _____
13. _____
14. _____
15. _____

Let's Talk With a partner, practice saying the amounts as your partner points to the different numbers.
Go as quickly as you can. See how many you can say in two minutes.

$0.57	$45.69	$234.67	$1,454.72	$23,876.23	$114,000.00
$1.34	$13.17	$129.54	$3,492.98	$18,752.09	$457,864.80
$0.08	$26.35	$869.19	$7,532.08	$49,897.99	$219,436.50
$2.31	$89.99	$724.34	$4,003.87	$96,832.34	$350,800.65
$5.69	$34.58	$367.23	$2,465.13	$75,000.45	$635,050.24
$8.37	$58.86	$712.14	$8,987.46	$37,559.90	$759,245.00

Listen: The /ae/ and /e/ sounds (1:15) Repeat after the speaker.

1. bat   bet
2. than   then
3. had   head

4. dad   dead
5. laughed   left
6. bag   beg

7. sad   said
8. man   men
9. pan   pen

Circle the word that you hear the speaker say in the sentences below.

1. This (pan / pen.) is too small to use.
2. His friends (laughed / left) when he arrived.
3. Do you want to make a (bat / bet)?
4. Did you see the (man / men) over there?
5. Let's put the (axe / X) over there.

Now take turns with a partner saying the sentences above. Choose a word to complete the sentence.

Lesson 5: An Old Man

Look at the picture below. Discuss what you think the story will be about.

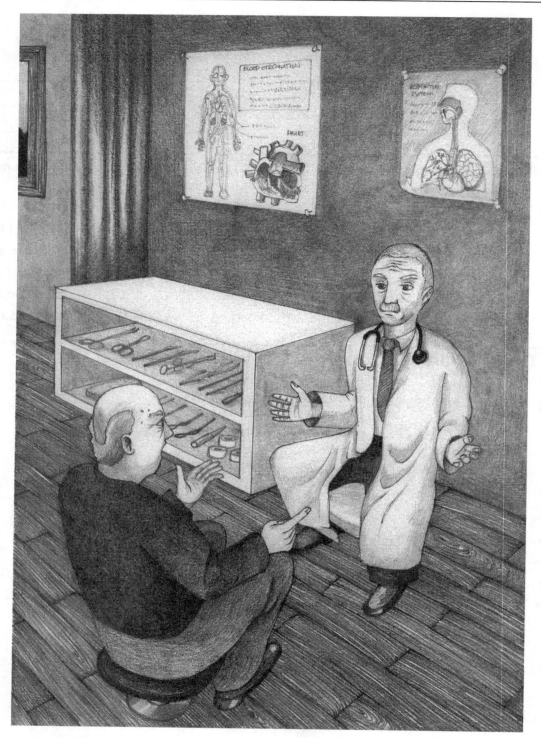

Biography and Background

Guy de Maupassant (1850-1893) is generally thought of as the greatest French short story writer. During the 1880s he wrote about 300 short stories, six novels, three travel books, and one book of poetry. Later he even wrote great horror stories. His short stories, such as **"An Old Man"** were often built around simple scenes from everyday life, and show hidden sides of people — sometimes very humorous.

An Old Man

By Guy De Maupassant

An old man moved into a city that was famous because people there lived long, long lives. This old man, Mr. Daron, was eighty-six years old, but always lied about his age. He was very healthy and tried in every way possible to avoid death. He was obsessed with staying alive. When he visited with the community doctor, he said, "I am in good health because I have lived very carefully. I keep free of illnesses, I exercise, and I eat right. I understand that this city is very good for the health. But before I decide to stay here permanently, I want proof. I would like you to see me once a week and tell me how all the people over the age of eighty are doing." The doctor agreed.

Mr. Daron avoided anything that would be considered fun. He lived a very strict lifestyle and kept mostly to himself. On the second visit, the doctor brought him a list with seventeen names of people living there who were over eighty.

Each week the doctor would report to Mr. Daron about the health of these seventeen people, and each week Mr. Daron would explain the causes and cures of their illnesses. One day the doctor announced as he sat down, "Rosalie Tournel has died."

"What was the cause?" inquired Mr. Daron.

"She died of a chill," replied the doctor. The old man gave a sigh of relief.

"She was overweight and must have eaten too much. When I get to her age, I'll be more careful about my weight." (He was actually two years older than she was, but he claimed to only be seventy.)

A few months later the doctor reported that Henry Brissot had died. Again Mr. Daron inquired how the man died.

"He died of pneumonia."

"Oh, well the man was obviously a fool then! At his age to go outside in the cold like that. I'll be much more careful than that. I guess that's life, though. The weakest people go first, and the strong ones go on."

Another two passed away during the year, one of dysentery and the other of a choking fit. Mr. Daron again blamed the deaths on the carelessness and foolishness of the individuals, and promised that he would not make the same mistakes.

But one evening the doctor announced that Paul Timonet, one of the healthiest men in the valley, had died.

"What did he die of?" asked Mr. Daron.

"I don't know."

"What do you mean you don't know? A doctor always knows. Was it some kind of infection?"

"No, none."

"Was his stomach functioning properly, did he have a stroke?"

"There was no stroke, and no problems with his organs."

"Look, the man obviously died of something!"

The doctor threw up his hands. "I have no idea what it was."

Then Mr. Daron asked, "How old was he?"

"Eighty-nine."

"Eighty-nine? So whatever it was, it wasn't old age..."

Vocabulary Find
Read through the story and circle any words or phrases that you don't understand. Discuss the words you circled and the vocabulary below with your teacher, or look them up in a dictionary.

obsessed	eat right	strict	pneumonia
community	permanently	cures	dysentery
avoid(ed)	proof	chill	a stroke

Expressions
Here are related expressions to the topic of the story: **LIFE/DEATH**. Review as a class.

1. *"He kicked the bucket."* (Impolite way to say that he died.)
2. *"She passed away last night."* (Polite way to say that she died last night.)
3. *"He's going to meet his maker."* (He is going to die and meet God in heaven.)
4. *"He said that he was dead tired."* (He was really tired.)
5. *"It's to die for."* (It's a wonderful thing or experience.)

Writing/Discussion
First, write short answers. Then discuss your answers in groups, or as a class.

1. Who were the main characters in the story? What do we know about them?

   _____

   _____

2. What did Mr. Daron want the doctor to do each week?

   _____

   _____

3. How many people died and what did Mr. Daron say about them?

   _____

   _____

4. Why was Mr. Daron's response about Mr. Timonet funny?

   _____

   _____

5. Do you know any people who are obsessed with certain things?

   _____

   _____

Listen: Vocabulary Fill-in (1:17)
First, choose and write the correct word in the sentences below. Then listen to the speakers to check your answers.

1. The people really liked the _____ a lot. They decided to stay.

   obsessed   community   avoided   permanently   proof

2. The man was _____ about getting sick. He wouldn't even leave the house.

   obsessed   community   avoided   permanently   proof

3. He needed _____ that the people were healthy before he would believe it.

   obsessed   community   avoided   permanently   proof

4. The people _____ the young man because he looked really angry.

   obsessed   community   avoided   permanently   proof

5. They decided to _____ stay in the small community.

   obsessed   community   avoided   permanently   proof

Let's Talk
Pretend that you are doctors. In small groups, talk about what you would and wouldn't do for each person. Then discuss your answers as a class with the teacher.

1. A young woman has a bad headache.
2. A young man's nose is bleeding and won't stop.
3. A little girl has cut her foot. The cut is pretty deep.
4. A little boy has a sore throat.
5. A man has a really bad case of the flu.
6. A woman has been in a swimming accident and isn't breathing.
7. A man has something in his eye.
8. A young boy has broken his arm.

Listen: Practice (1-18)
Listen to each situation. Decide what the problem is with each person.

PERSON	PROBLEM
1. **Brian**	a. He has a runny nose and is sick.
	b. He has a broken nose from fighting.
	c. He has a bloody nose which won't stop bleeding.
2. **Sharon**	a. She has the flu and feels very weak.
	b. She has a bad cold and can't stop sneezing.
	c. She has a bad headache that won't go away.
3. **William**	a. He thinks that he broke his arm.
	b. He thinks that he broke his leg.
	c. He thinks that he broke his wrist.
4. **Kathryn**	a. She has a bad stomach ache.
	b. She has a bad tooth ache.
	c. She says that her back really aches.
5. **Cindy**	a. She feels cold all over and can't get warm.
	b. She feels too hot and can't cool down.
	c. She feels nervous and can't calm down.
6. **Greg**	a. He cut his foot really badly.
	b. He cut his hand really badly.
	c. He cut his leg really badly.
7. **Robert**	a. His throat is sore.
	b. The insides of his ears hurt.
	c. His eyes are bothering him.

Listen: The /u/ and /oo/ sounds (1:19)
Repeat after the speaker.

1. full   fool
2. pull   pool
3. look   Luke
4. soot   suit
5. bucks   books
6. ton   tune
7. son   soon
8. dumb   doom
9. guns   goons

Circle the word that you hear the speaker say in the sentences below.

1. He said that he was a little (full / fool).
2. The sign said (pull / pool) on the door.
3. I need to borrow ten (bucks / books) from you.
4. I think we'd better leave (son / soon).
5. (Look / Luke), the answer is simple if you'd listen to me.

Now take turns with a partner saying the sentences above. Choose a word to complete the sentence.

Lesson 6: The Cat That Walked by Himself

Look at the picture below. Discuss what you think the story will be about.

Biography and Background

Rudyard Kipling (1865-1936) was the first English writer to win the Nobel Prize for literature. His novels and poetry are read by adults, but both adults and children have always loved his *Just So Stories*, which includes *"The Cat That Walked by Himself."*

The Cat That Walked by Himself

By Rudyard Kipling

There was a time in the past when the tame animals were wild. The dog was wild, as was the horse, and the cow, and the sheep and the pigs. The cat was the wildest of them all. He walked by himself, and all places seemed good to him.

Man was wild, too. At night man and woman would sit together in their cave and cook sheep, duck, and pork. Out in the woods, the wild animals gathered together each night where they could see the light of the fire and wondered what it was.

"Oh my friends and my enemies," said the horse. "why have the man and woman made light in that cave? What will it do to us?"

The dog smelled the meat that the man and woman were cooking and had an idea. "I will go up and see what they are doing. Cat, come with me."

"No," said the cat. I am the cat who walks by himself, and all places seem good to me. I will not go with you."

"Then we can never be friends again," said Wild Dog, and he walked toward the cave. The cat secretly followed behind the dog.

When the dog reached the cave, he smelled something wonderful.

"Oh my enemy and wife of my enemy, what is this that smells so good?" asked the dog.

The woman picked up a bone with meat on it and threw it to the dog. The dog ate the meat and looked at the woman. "Please give me another."

"If you will help my man hunt throughout the day and guard this cave at night, I will give you bones and meat every day." Wild Dog agreed and went into the cave to join them.

"Ah, said the cat. That is a very foolish dog," and he went back into the woods alone.

The next night the woman had cut green grass and left it lying by the fire. Out in the woods, the wild animals wondered what happened to Wild Dog. The horse said, "I will go and see why Wild Dog has not returned. Cat, will you come with me?"

"No," said the cat. "I am the cat who walks by himself, and all places seem good to me." But secretly he followed Wild Horse up to the cave.

The horse walked up to the cave. "Oh my enemy and wife of my enemy, where is Wild Dog?" The woman laughed, and said, "You are not here to see Wild Dog, but to eat the grass that I have placed by the fire."

"The grass looks very good to me. Give me some to eat."

"If you will carry heavy things that I give you to carry, you shall eat grass three times a day."

"I will carry heavy things for you if you give me grass three times a day," said the horse. And he remained outside the cave.

"Ah," said the cat. "That is a very foolish horse, and he went back into the woods alone.

The next day the Wild Cow came to the cave, and the cat secretly followed behind. The woman promised the cow fresh hay in exchange for milk. The cow agreed.

"That is a very foolish cow," said the cat, and he went back into the woods alone.

The next day the Wild Cat decided to go to the cave. The woman looked at Wild Cat and said,

"We have no need for you. We have all the animals we need. You are neither a friend, nor a servant."

"Is there nothing I can do to enter into the cave and enjoy the warmth of the fire and the taste of the cow's milk?' asked the cat.

The woman responded, "If I ever say one good thing about you, you may enter the cave."

"And if you should say two good things about me?" asked the cat.

"If I ever say two good things about you, you may sit by the fire."

"And if you should say three good things about me?" asked the cat.

"I never will, but if I should say three good things about you, you may drink the cow's milk while sitting by the fire." The cat agreed. He watched and waited patiently outside the cave for many days. The woman had forgotten the promise she had made to the cat...

Vocabulary Find
Read through the story and circle any words or phrases that you don't understand. Discuss the words you circled and the vocabulary below with your teacher, or look them up in a dictionary.

tame	enemy(ies)	grass	wild
cave	bone(s)	hay	pork
woods	guard	servant	secret(ly)

Expressions
Here are related expressions to the topic of the story: **ANIMALS**. Review as a class.

1. *"I heard it straight from the horse's mouth."* (I heard it from someone who really knows.)
2. *"She has the appetite of a bird."* (She doesn't eat very much.)
3. *"Holy cow!"* (I don't believe it.)
4. *"Every dog has his day."* (Every person gets lucky sometimes.)
5. *"He's a strong as an ox."* (He is very strong.)

Writing/Discussion
First, write short answers. Then discuss your answers in groups, or as a class.

1. Who were the main characters in the story? What do we know about them?

   _____

   _____

2. Why did the animals want to go into the cave?

   _____

   _____

3. Why didn't the cat join the other animals?

   _____

   _____

4. What does the woman say to the cat?

   _____

   _____

5. What do you think will happen next?

   _____

   _____

Vocabulary Match
Match the vocabulary word to its definition. Work in pairs or as a class.

tame	an opening or hole inside a large rock or mountain
cave	another name for forest or group of trees
woods	a person or group of people who are fighting against another person or group
enemy	not wild, a domesticated animal, or an animal that is friendly to humans
bone	to protect from danger
guard	green plant that grows very short
grass	a hard structures of an animal's body, the framework of a body
hay	someone who serves another
servant	meat that comes from a pig
wild	a plant that grows very long and is cut and fed to animals
pork	without anyone knowing, hidden, not easily seen
secretly	not tame, not being controlled or friendly to humans

Listen: Practice (1:21) Listen to the following people describe the pets that they have. Write down the name of the animal(s) that each person has.

Jack

Karen

Mike

Sharon

_____

_____

_____

_____

_____

_____

_____

_____

_____

_____

_____

_____

Let's Talk Discuss the following questions in small groups or as a class.

1. What pets have you had before? Describe them.

2. What animals make the best pets?

3. What animals make the worst pets?

4. What was the strangest pet you have ever seen?

5. What are common pets in your home country?

6. What have you noticed are common pets where you live now?

Listen: The /ae/ and /o/ sounds (1:22) Repeat after the speaker.

1. cat cot	4. pat pot	7. bag bog
2. bat bought	5. fat fought	8. Mack mock
3. rad rod	6. rack rock	9. saggy soggy

Circle the word that you hear the speaker say in the sentences below.

1. The boy saw a (rack / rock) sitting outside the store.

2. The young girl received a (pat / pot) from her mother.

3. That's a pretty large (bag / bog).

4. He accidentally sat down on the (cat / cot).

5. The sign in the window said (bat / bought).

Now take turns with a partner saying the sentences above. Choose a word to complete the sentence.

Look at the picture below. Discuss what you think the story will be about.

...the cat chased after the string and played with it.

The Cat Who Walked By Himself (continued)

By Rudyard Kipling

One day the baby started crying and would not stop. The cat walked to the baby and rubbed its warm, soft body around the baby's arms, and the baby stopped crying.

"Thank you Wild Animal, for doing this," said the woman.

The cat entered into the cave and sat down. "You have spoken one good thing about me, so I shall stay in the cave."

Days later the baby cried and would not stop. The cat told the woman to give him a bit of string and he would make the baby start laughing instead of crying. The woman gave the cat the string, and the cat chased after the string and played with it in such a way that the baby began to laugh. He then rubbed his soft fur around the baby's body until the baby fell asleep.

"That was wonderful," said the woman, and the cat sat down by the warmth of the fire. A few days later a mouse wandered into the cave.

'If I eat up the mouse, will you be grateful?" asked the cat.

"Yes, if you eat up the mouse, I will be grateful," replied the woman. The cat caught the mouse and ate it up. The woman was very pleased. "You are a very clever animal, perhaps the wisest animal I have seen."

He went over to the bowl of milk and began drinking.

"You promised that I could have milk if you complimented me three times," said the cat.

"Yes, but remember that the man and the dog have not made any bargains with you. I do not know what they will do when they get home."

When they arrived, the man told the cat that if he did not catch mice, he would throw things at him. The dog said that if the cat was not kind to the baby he would chase him and bite him. The cat agreed.

"But still I am the cat that walks by himself and all places seem good to me," said the cat.

One day, the man became angry and threw things at the cat. The dog also became angry and chased the cat up a tree. Even today, most men will throw things at a cat, and most dogs will chase a cat up a tree. The cat still kills mice and will be kind to babies, but when he is not doing that, he is the cat that walks by himself and all places seem good to him.

Vocabulary Find
Read through the story and circle any words or phrases that you don't understand. Discuss the words you circled and the vocabulary below with your teacher, or look them up in a dictionary.

grateful	chased	pleased	bargain(s)
rubbed	fur	clever	wisest
string	mouse	complimented	bite

Expressions
Here are related expressions to the topic of the story: **CATS**. Review as a class.

1. *"Don't let the cat out of the bag."* (Don't tell anyone our secret.)
2. *"It's raining cats and dogs outside."* (It's really raining hard outside.)
3. *"That guy is the cat's meow."* (That man is really a great person.)
4. *"You must have nine lives."* (You were lucky to survive: A cat has nine lives.)
5. *"...cat got your tongue?"* (Don't you have anything to say?)

Writing/Discussion
First, write short answers. Then discuss your answers in groups, or as a class.

1. Who were the main characters in the story? What do we know about them?

_____

_____

2. What was the first thing that the cat did to receive a reward?

_____

_____

3. What was the second thing the cat did, and what was the reward?

_____

_____

4. What was the third thing the cat did, and what was the reward?

_____

_____

5. What happened to the cat in the end?

_____

_____

Listen: Vocabulary Fill-in (2:2)
First, choose and write the correct word in the sentences below. Then listen to the speakers to check your answers.

1. The cat _____ itself against the baby's skin and it stopped crying.

    grateful   rubbed   string   chased   fur

2. The _____ woman began shaking hands and saying "thank you" to everyone.

    grateful   rubbed   string   chased   fur

3. The cat played with some _____ that was lying around on the floor.

    grateful   rubbed   string   chased   fur

4. The cat had a lot of _____ that was warm and soft.

    grateful   rubbed   string   chased   fur

5. The cat _____ the mouse all around the bedroom.

    grateful   rubbed   string   chased   fur

6. The boy was _____ with his progress in the class.

    pleased   **clever**   **bite**   **bargain**   **complimented**

7. The woman _____ the small boy on how well he played the violin.

    pleased   **clever**   **bite**   **bargain**   **complimented**

8. The dog tried to _____ the man on the leg.

    pleased   **clever**   **bite**   **bargain**   **complimented**

Let's Talk ABC in the cave. In groups or as a class take turns completing the sentence, adding another item to the list, following the alphabet.

Example: "I'm looking in the cave, and I see a(n) apple."

"I'm looking in the cave, and I see an apple, and a ball."

"I'm looking in the cave, and I see an apple, a ball, and a cat..."

A B C D E F G H I J K L M N O P Q R S T U V W X Y Z

Listen: Practice (2:3) Where is the cat? Listen to the speakers as they describe where the cat is. Write down the number under the appropriate picture.

Listen: The /or/ and /er/ sounds (2:4) Repeat after the speaker.

1. ward	word	4.	torn	turn	7.	stor	stir	
2. four	fur	5.	born	burn	8.	bored	bird	
3. shorts	shirts	6.	sore	sir	9.	for	firm	

Circle the word that you hear the speaker say in the sentences below.

1. Her mother told her she should (store / stir) the soup.
2. They went to the mall to buy some (shorts / shirts).
3. I think you have the wrong (ward / word).
4. She said that she wanted (four / fur).
5. He told us that it was a nice (form / firm).

Now take turns with a partner saying the sentences above. Choose a word to complete the sentence.

Lesson 8: The Little Trick

Look at the picture below. Discuss what you think the story will be about.

Biography and Background

Anton Chekhov (1860-1904) As a medical student in Russia, Chekhov began writing short stories to help support his family. He became a doctor, but he is remembered as a major playwright and a master of the short story. *"The Little Trick"* is an example of his inventiveness.

The Little Trick

By Anton Chekhov

It was winter and I was with Nadyenka. We had a toboggan ready to go down a steep hill.

"Let's go down, Nadyenka," I asked her. "Just one time. I promise that it's safe." She looked at me and I could see the terror in her eyes. She was afraid. The hill seemed too steep to control the toboggan, and I knew that she didn't want to go.

"Please come!" I said. "There's no need to be afraid." She finally gave in, but I could see that she was very scared, so I held on to her tight and told her to hold onto the toboggan tight. Off we went, down the hill. The cold air hit us in the face, it whistled in our ears, and bit at our ears. Faster and faster we went. We were almost out of control. Just when it appeared that we would lose control, I said in a low voice, "I love you Nadya."

The toboggan began to slow down and we finally stopped at the base of the hill. No longer was the cold wind hitting us straight on. We survived the trip. Nadya's face was white and she was barely breathing. I helped her to her feet.

"I wouldn't do that again for anything!" she said. "Not for anything in the world! We nearly killed ourselves!" After a few minutes, she began to look at me. She was questioning whether or not I spoke those four words. She took my arm and we walked a little bit, talking casually. But still, when she looked at me I could tell that she wanted so badly to know whether or not I spoke to her during the toboggan ride. I wasn't going to say a word about it.

"Let's take one more ride," she said to me.

"Are you sure?" I asked. I was playing with her. I knew the reason why she wanted to go for another ride, and it was not because she enjoyed tobogganing. Up the hill we marched, then as we were sailing down the hill again, just at the moment when we were almost out of control, I said in a low voice, "I love you, Nadyenka!"

When the toboggan stopped, she looked back up the hill, then at me. She seemed puzzled. She wanted to know, but could not bring herself to ask me the question. And on her face it was written: Did he say those words to me or was it the wind? The mystery was getting to her.

"Do you think we should go home?" I asked.

"Well, I like tobogganing. Let's go again." I could tell by the fear in her eyes that it was not the tobogganing that kept her here. Again we went down, again we almost lost control and again I said in a low voice, "I love you Nadya!"

The next morning I received a note, which said, "If you are going tobogganing again today, I would like to join you." So again the rush of cold air and the "I love you, Nadya". She still could not tell whether it was I or whether it was the wind. Each day for weeks we went up together and I played with her.

One day she decided to go down the hill alone. I wondered what would happen without me to whisper to her. Down the hill she went and when she finally stopped, I couldn't tell from her expression whether or not she received an answer.

Winter ended, and with it the tobogganing. No longer would Nadya hear the words, "I love you." I went off to Petersburg that summer, and never saw her again. Nadyenka married and had children. She did not forget the time we went tobogganing together long ago, and that the wind carried to her the words, "I love you, Nadyenka." It may have been the happiest, most beautiful moment in her life. Even now, I cannot understand why I said those words to her, nor why I played the little trick.

Vocabulary Find
Read through the story and circle any words or phrases that you don't understand. Discuss the words you circled and the vocabulary below with your teacher, or look them up in a dictionary.

toboggan	whistled	marched	wind
steep	base of the hill	sailing	expression
terror	casually	puzzled	trick

Expressions
Here are related expressions to the topic of the story: **LOVE**. Review as a class..

1. *"Love makes the world go round."* (Love is a very important thing.)
2. *"He is head over heels for Susan."* (He really loves Susan.)
3. *"She was just walking on air after the date with Daniel."* (She fell in love with Daniel.)
4. *"Love is blind."* (Love will accept things as they are.)
5. *"I've fallen for you."* (I've grown to love you.)

Writing/Discussion
First, write short answers. Then discuss your answers in groups, or as a class.

1. Who were the main characters in the story? What do we know about them?

_____

_____

2. What was the girl afraid of?

_____

_____

3. Why did she continue to toboggan down the hill?

_____

_____

4. What was the mystery that Nadya wanted to discover?

_____

_____

5. Do you think the trick was a good trick or a bad trick? Why?

_____

_____

Vocabulary Match
Match the vocabulary word to its definition. Work in pairs or as a class.

toboggan	extreme fright
steep	a kind of sled for going down snowy hills
terror	a high sound, or a sound made by blowing
whistled	nearly straight up or straight down (as a hill)
casually	to walk with a purpose, or to walk together in step
march	not strict or formal, very loose and easy
sailing	a joke played on someone to fool them
puzzled	moving along easily and quickly (usually in a boat)
expression	not able to understand, confused
trick	an emotion or look on one's face

Listen: Practice (2:6) Listen to the speakers. Write down the name of the person next to the activity that he/she loves to do.

1. _____ Loves to go skiing during winter.

2. _____ Loves to go dancing on weekends.

3. _____ Loves to go to the beach for a vacation.

4. _____ Loves to watch movies with friends.

5. _____ Loves to go out to nice restaurants to eat.

6. _____ Loves to play basketball with friends.

Let's Talk Find someone in the classroom who likes to do the following things. Have each person sign his or her name by the activity that he/she likes to do.

Do you like to . . .

_____ watch scary movies at night? Explain why.

_____ go for long bike rides? Explain why.

_____ play computer games? Explain why.

_____ read the newspaper every day? Explain why.

_____ listen to music on the radio? Explain why.

_____ work out every day at a gym? Explain why.

_____ just sit and talk to people? Explain why.

_____ learn a foreign language? Explain why.

Listen: The /ar/ and /er/ sounds (2:7) Repeat after the speaker.

1. far	fur	4. star	stir	7. cards	curds
2. barn	burn	5. heart	hurt	8. quark	quirk
3. hard	heard	6. yarn	yearn	9. farm	firm

Circle the word that you hear the speaker say in the sentences below.

1. I don't think it is (far / fur).

2. She didn't think her speech was (hard / heard).

3. The children were looking at the (cards / curds).

4. He was looking for the (barn / burn) in the picture.

5. The doctor was worried about the girl's (heart / hurt) muscles.

Now take turns with a partner saying the sentences above. Choose a word to complete the sentence.

Lesson 9: The Gift of the Magi

Look at the picture below. Discuss what you think the story will be about.

Biography and Background

This story by **O. Henry** is probably his most famous. Like his other stories, **"The Gift of the Magi"** has an ending that brings a surprise to the reader. It will also bring a smile to your lips and a tear to your eyes when you finish reading.

The Gift of the Magi

By O. Henry

One dollar and eighty-seven cents. That was all. And sixty cents of it was in pennies. Pennies saved one and two at a time for months and months. Three times Della counted it. James and Della Dillingham were having tough times recently. But whenever James came home, Della was there with a hug and a kiss. At least they had love, and that was enough for them.

Tomorrow would be Christmas Day. Even after saving for months she still had less than two dollars to spend for her husband's Christmas gift. As she looked at herself in the mirror, she got an idea. She pulled down her long, beautiful hair and let it fall to its full length.

There were two possessions of the Dillinghams which they both took pride in. One was a gold watch that James had inherited from his father, and his father from his father. The other was Della's hair. She looked at her beautiful hair in the mirror. Quickly she put on her coat and hat and went out the door, down the stairs, and into the street. She stopped at a sign: Madame Sofronie — Hair Goods of all Kinds — Wigs.

"Will you buy my hair?" asked Della.

"I buy hair. Take off your hat and let's have a look at it."

Off came the hat and down came the beautiful hair.

"I'll give you twenty dollars for it."

"Agreed," said Della, with tears in her eyes.

For the next two hours she searched through many different stores for James' present. She found it at last. It was a gold chain for his watch. It would make the watch look so much nicer than the leather strap that he used. She paid the twenty dollars and quickly hurried home.

She tried to arrange her hair so that James would not notice it, but it was no use. At seven o'clock James arrived, removed his coat and hat and sat down in the living room. When he looked at Della, he fixed his eyes upon her hair.

"I just had to get you a gift for Christmas, James! I sold my hair, and with the money I bought you a nice Christmas gift. Please tell me you understand!"

James took a small package from his pocket and placed it on the table.

"I don't have any problem with your hair, Della. I love you no matter what. It's just that, well, when you open my present to you, you'll understand my surprise."

She opened the box carefully. Inside was a set of beautiful combs and brushes.

"My hair grows so fast, James. This is a wonderful gift. I don't know how you could afford such beautiful combs and brushes." She brought out her gift and handed it to James. He opened it up and stared at the gold chain inside the box.

"I hunted all over town to find it. Isn't it wonderful? Let's see how it looks with your watch!" James put the lid back on the box and set it on the table. He smiled lovingly at his wife.

"It's a wonderful gift, Della. I'll put it away for a while and use it when I get another watch. You see, I sold my gold watch to buy you the combs and brushes."

He gave her a hug and a kiss, as tears came into his eyes. At least they had love, and it was enough for them.

Vocabulary Find
Read through the story and circle any words or phrases that you don't understand. Discuss the words you circled and the vocabulary below with your teacher, or look them up in a dictionary.

pennies	inherited	strap	combs
mirror	chain	arrange	brushes
possessions	leather	wig	lid

Expressions
Here are related expressions to the topic of the story: **SACRIFICE**. Review as a class.

1. *"He would give you the shirt off his back."* (He is so generous.)
2. *"She has a heart of gold."* (She is such a nice person.)
3. *"He gave 110 percent."* (He tried / worked very hard.)
4. *"She put her whole heart into it."* (She put all her energy into it.)
5. *"He burned the midnight oil to get it done."* (He stayed up all night to finish it.)

Writing/Discussion
First, write short answers. Then discuss your answers in groups, or as a class.

1. Who were the main characters in the story? What do we know about them?

   _____

   _____

2. What did Della do to get James a Christmas gift?

   _____

   _____

3. What did James do to get Della a gift?

   _____

   _____

4. Why were the gifts special?

   _____

   _____

5. Do you know anyone who has sacrificed a lot to make others happy?

   _____

   _____

Listen: Vocabulary Fill-in (2:9)
First, choose and write the correct word in the sentences below. Then listen to the speakers to check your answers.

1. The man had to wear a _____ because he was losing his hair.

   pennies   mirror   possessions   wig   brushes

2. There were many different kinds of _____ on the counter to style her hair.

   pennies   mirror   possessions   wig   brushes

3. She looked at herself in the _____ as she was combing her hair.

   pennies   mirror   possessions   wig   brushes

4. The little boy counted fifteen _____ in his glass jar.

   pennies   mirror   possessions   wig   brushes

5. They didn't have very many _____ in their house.

   pennies   mirror   possessions   wig   brushes

6. The woman took the _____ off the bottle and poured out the juice.

   leather   lid   combs   mirror   pennies

7. There were many different kinds of _____ on the table at the beauty salon.

   leather   lid   combs   mirror   pennies

Let's Talk: Island Sacrifice Read the information below and decide as a group what to do.

You and your group members are lost on an island in the middle of the ocean. It has been over three weeks and nobody has found you. You have used up almost all of your supplies. You decide that you will not survive much longer, so you are going to leave the island. You have the following items with you:

    a life raft big enough for your group members
    a five-gallon container filled with fresh water
    a compass
    a small mirror
    six candy bars
    two bottles of whisky (alcohol)
    a box of matches
    a bottle of suntan lotion
    a book on survival skills
    a loaded gun
    a pocket lighter
    a hand radio
    a flashlight
    some fishing poles with lures

Your life raft does not have enough room for everything. Decide which 5 items are the most important. You will take these five items with you. You will leave the other items on the island. Which items will you take with you and why? Work in groups of 3 or 4, then as a class. Explain the choices you made.

Group decision

1. _____
2. _____
3. _____
4. _____
5. _____

Class decision

1. _____
2. _____
3. _____
4. _____
5. _____

Listen: The /u/ and /er/ sounds (2:10) Repeat after the speaker.

1. shut	shirt	4. buns	burns	7. cub	curb
2. huts	hurts	5. buds	birds	8. fun	fern
3. thud	third	6. gulls	girls	9. ton	turn

Circle the word that you hear the speaker say in the sentences below.

1. The big tree was covered with (buds / birds).

2. Look at all the (gulls / girls) on the beach.

3. They were looking for a little (fun / fern).

4. The people were looking at the (buns / burns).

5. The little boy saw the (cub / curb) from the tour bus.

Now take turns with a partner saying the sentences above. Choose a word to complete the sentence.

Lesson 10: The Great Stone Face

Look at the picture below. Discuss what you think the story will be about.

Biography and Background

Nathaniel Hawthorne (1804-1864) Hawthorne is recognized as one of America's most important writers. His work falls somewhere between the real world and the imaginary. He felt that imagination works to create the world we live in. He was deeply interested in moral issues, as the story *"The Great Stone Face"* will show.

Listen: Comprehension (2:11) Listen to the story.

Option 1: Read along in your book.   Option 2: Listen to the story with your book closed.

The Great Stone Face

by Nathaniel Hawthorne

One afternoon, as the sun was going down, a mother and her little boy sat and looked at the mountain that the town called The Great Stone Face. They called it that because the rocks formed the shape of a man's face. As they were looking at the mountain, Ernest, the young boy, said, "I wish that the man in the mountain could speak. It looks like such a kind and respectable man. If I met a man with a face like that I'm sure I would love him dearly."

"There is a prophecy—something people believe will happen—about this," answered his mother. So his mother told him a story that her own parents had told her when she was a little girl. The story stated that some day in the future a child born here would become the greatest and most respected man in the valley. His face would resemble the face on the mountain.

"Oh, Mother, I hope that I shall live to see him someday!"

"Perhaps you will someday, Ernest."

Ernest never forgot the story. He grew to become a hard-working, intelligent young man. Ernest gazed at The Great Stone Face every day after finishing his work. He began to imagine that the mountain was his friend. He hoped for the day when he could meet the great man who resembled the mountain.

Some years later a rumor spread throughout the valley that a man named Mr. Gathergold might be the person the valley citizens were looking for. Mr. Gathergold was a clever man who had earned a lot of money. He liked nothing better than making money and spending it on a luxurious lifestyle. Still, people in the community believed that he was the Stone Face they had all been waiting to see.

When Ernest saw the old man, he was disappointed. He had none of the qualities of the Great Stone Face. Instead of being generous, the old man kept all his money to himself. Instead of helping people, he ignored them. As Ernest looked up at the mountain, it seemed to tell him, "He will come, Ernest. The man will come!"

As the years went by Ernest mostly went unnoticed among the townspeople, except that everyone knew that he still gazed up at the mountain every evening. What they did not realize was that the Great Stone Face had become Ernest's teacher. Ernest had learned to become industrious, kind, and neighborly. He remained a simple man, as simple as when his mother first taught him the old prophecy, a prophecy that Earnest still waited to see come true.

By this time, Mr. Gathergold had died a poor, lonely old man. The people stopped honoring him as The Great Stone Face, and simply called him Old Mr. Gathergold. So the people began to talk about when and if a man would enter the valley who would become the true Great Stone Face.

It happened that a man born in the valley had become a famous soldier and commander. This old war veteran returned home after being gone for a long time. His old neighbors and the rest of the valley decided that this man was The Great Stone Face that they had been waiting for. Many of the people in the valley stated that this man did, indeed, look like the famous mountain. They gave the old man a hero's welcome and began calling him The Great Stone Face. However, as Ernest looked at the old man, and at the mountain, he concluded that this was not the man that was prophesied to come.

"Fear not, Ernest," the mountain seemed to call to him. "Fear not, he will come."

More years passed, and Ernest was now middle-aged. By then, people of the valley knew him for his honesty and integrity. He was now very well-respected in the community. It seemed that every day he was doing some service for someone in need. He became a preacher, and used the teachings of the mountain to inspire the members of the community who came to listen to him. He taught the people wonderful things that endeared him to them.

The old soldier died, and with him died the title of The Great Stone Face. The citizens of the community realized that the commander did little to inspire the people, and they began to look for the great man who would become The Great Stone Face. Ernest was among those who waited and watched patiently for him to come...

Vocabulary Find

Read through the story and circle any words or phrases that you don't understand. Discuss the words you circled and the vocabulary below with your teacher, or look them up in a dictionary.

rocks	prophecy	gaze	rumor
respectable	luxurious	industrious	inspire
dearly	valley	resembled	soldier

Expressions

Here are related expressions to the topic of the story: **HOPE**. Review as a class.

1. *"It's not over until the fat lady sings."* (There is still a chance of winning.)

2. *"I'll just have to hang in there."* (I'll just have to keep on trying.)

3. *"She said she was just about at the end of her rope."* (She said she is ready to quit.)

4. *"Our backs are against the wall."* (We are in a difficult situation.)

5. *"This is a real long shot, but we can still try it."* (This probably won't work.)

Writing/Discussion

First, write short answers. Then discuss your answers in groups, or as a class.

1. Who were the main characters in the story? What do we know about them?

_____

_____

2. What was the Great Stone Face?

_____

_____

3. What were the people in the valley waiting and hoping for?

_____

_____

4. What relationship does Ernest have with the Great Stone Face?

_____

_____

5. What do you think will happen?

_____

_____

Listen: Practice (2:12)

Listen to the speaker. Fill in the blanks with the words you hear.

Ernest never forgot the _____ about the Great Stone Face. He grew to become a hard-working, _____ young man. Ernest _____ at The Great Stone Face every day after finishing his _____ . He began to imagine that the _____ was his friend. He hoped for the day when he could meet the great _____ who resembled the mountain. He knew that he would _____ the man dearly.

Vocabulary Match Match the vocabulary word to its definition. Work in pairs or as a class.

respectable	a prediction of something to happen in the future
prophecy	a low area surrounded by hills and mountains
valley	being honored and admired by others
luxurious	to stare or to look at
gaze	very rich and good quality
resemble	a story that is passed on from one person to another
rumor	a person who fights in battles of war
soldier	to look like or to be similar in some way
industrious	working very hard

Let's Talk Work in groups of three. Take turns reading a paragraph, then discuss the questions.

I need some advice.

I am a college student. I have worked very hard the past three years and will graduate in one more year. My roommates and I are members of a rock music band. We play at local restaurants and bars. I enjoy playing music, but I also make sure that I have enough time for school. My roommates have already dropped out of school. They want to spend all their time playing music.

Recently, someone from the city heard us play at a bar and said that we should move to the city and that he would help us get our music on the radio and also help us to play in front of big groups of people. He said that if we are lucky, we will become rich and famous. He said that we might have the right kind of music to become successful, but that it may not work. It is taking a risk, because we may fail and end up losing all our money and time. My friends want me to drop out of college and join them.

I have always dreamed of playing our music in front of thousands of screaming fans. It would be a dream come true to become a member of a famous rock music band. The other members of the group have already decided to move to the city. They said that if I don't join them they will find someone else to take my place. Should I take the risk, drop out of school and join the band, or should I play it safe and stay in college? What would you do?

1. Who is writing for advice? What is the problem?
2. What do you think the person should do?
3. What are the consequences if he stays or if he goes?
4. Do you like to take risks, or do you prefer to play it safe?

Listen: The /t/ and /d/ sounds (2:13) Repeat after the speaker.

1. tall	doll	4. two	do	7. train	drain
2. bat	bad	5. cart	card	8. time	dime
3. heart	hard	6. write	ride	9. tore	door

Circle the word that you hear the speaker say in the sentences below.

1. Do you want to (try / dry) this shirt?
2. The people were looking at the problems with the (train / drain).
3. He was looking at the (cart / card).
4. Jeremy was a (bat / bad) boy this summer.
5. Do you want to (write / ride) with the rest of us?

Now take turns with a partner saying the sentences above. Choose a word to complete the sentence.

Look the picture below. Discuss what you think the story will be about.

The two of them went to the center of town, where Ernest was to give a sermon to the people.

Listen: Comprehension (2:14) Listen to the story.

Option 1: Read along in your book.   **Option 2:** Listen to the story with your book closed.

The Great Stone Face (continued)

by Nathaniel Hawthorne

More years passed, and a young man, born in the valley, moved away and was now a famous politician. He was so popular that his political party nominated him to run for president. While his friends were doing their best to make him president, the young man returned to visit the valley where he was born. The people were very excited. They believed that finally The Great Stone Face was going to fulfill the prophecy. But the young man cared little about his hometown, and before the citizens knew it, he had made his speech, asked for their votes, and was on his way.

The townspeople were disappointed, especially Ernest. But as he looked up at the mountain, it seemed to say to him, "Here I am, Earnest. I have waited longer than you, and am not yet tired. Fear not, the man will come."

With the passing years, Earnest became more and more respected in the valley as a very wise man. College professors, leaders of cities, and other important individuals came from far away to converse with him. His fame for deep thinking and ideas unlike those of any other man began to spread far and wide. Ernest spoke with these people with kindness, sincerity, and from his heart. Upon leaving the valley the individuals looked up at the Great Stone Face. They imagined that they had seen that same face in human form, but could not remember where.

One day a poet visited the small valley. Ernest had read his poetry and was impressed. It happened that the poet had also heard of Earnest, and had thought much about him. He wanted very much to meet this wonderful man. Arriving at Ernest's house, he found him there reading a book and looking up at the mountain from time to time.

"Good evening," said the poet. "Can you give a traveler a room for the night?"

"Absolutely," replied Ernest. The poet sat down on the bench beside him and the two of them talked about many things. The poet was deeply impressed by the thoughts and feelings that Ernest presented to him. Earnest was also impressed with the poet.

"Who are you, my friend?" Ernest asked. The poet took the book that Ernest had been reading and pointed at one of the pages.

"You have read these poems. I wrote them." Ernest looked at the poet and then at the Great Stone Face, then back at the poet. There was a look of disappointment in his face.

"Why are you sad?" asked the poet.

"I was hoping that you would fulfill a prophecy."

"You hoped, " responded the poet, "that I would have the look of the Great Stone Face. Now you are disappointed, just as you were with the other three men who came before me."

The two of them went to the center of town, where Ernest was to give a sermon to the people. As he spoke, the poet noticed something about his face. He looked at Ernest, and then at the Great Stone Face, then back at Ernest. When Ernest had finished talking, the poet stood up and said,

"Look here, good people! Ernest, himself, has the likeness of the Great Stone Face!" Then all the people looked and saw that the poet was correct. The prophecy was fulfilled! Earnest finished what he had to say, took the poet's arm, and walked home. He never stopped hoping that some wiser and better man than himself would appear, someone having the likeness of the Great Stone Face.

Vocabulary Find
Read through the story and circle any words or phrases that you don't understand. Discuss the words you circled and the vocabulary below with your teacher, or look them up in a dictionary.

popular	fame	poet	fulfill
politician	spread	likeness	disappointment
nominated	sincerely	bench	sermon

Expressions
Here are related expressions to the topic of the story: **SERVICE**. Review as a class.

1. *"He's all heart."* (He works very hard for others.)
2. *"She worked her (head / tail) off."* (She worked very hard.)
3. *"Can I give you a hand with that?"* (Can I help you?)
4. *"He has a hard time pulling his own weight."* (He has a hard time doing his job.)
5. *"Don't bite off more than you can chew."* (Don't try to do too much at one time.)

Writing/Discussion
First, write short answers. Then discuss your answers in groups, or as a class.

1. What other characters are involved in this part of the story?

   _____

   _____

2. What happens to Ernest?

   _____

   _____

3. Why doesn't Ernest ever meet the man who is the Great Stone Face?

   _____

   _____

4. How would you describe the change in Ernest?

   _____

   _____

5. How does the story end?

   _____

   _____

Listen: Vocabulary Fill-in (2:15)
First, choose and write the correct word in the sentences below. Then listen to the speakers to check your answers.

1. The famous _____ gave a good speech to the people.

   popular   politician   fame   sincerely   poet   bench

2. The man was _____ concerned about the happiness of the people.

   popular   politician   fame   sincerely   poet   bench

3. The _____ gave some interesting stories about love and respect.

   popular   politician   fame   sincerely   poet   bench

4. The two men sat down on a _____ and talked for a while.

   popular   politician   fame   sincerely   poet   bench

5. The boy was the most _____ person in his whole class.

   popular   politician   fame   sincerely   poet   bench

6. The man's _____ was known throughout the whole community.

    popular   politician   fame   sincerely   poet   bench

7. The news about the woman _____ throughout the neighborhood.

    spread   fame   sincerely   poet   bench   popular

Let's Talk Work with a partner. The teacher will write a letter of the alphabet on the board. Find the following kinds of words that begin with that letter. Compete as teams to see who finishes each one first.

> **Starts With The Letter _____**
>
> **Name** _____
> **Country** _____
> **Color** _____
> **Fruit/Vegetable** _____
> **Animal** _____
> **Job** _____
> **Verb** _____
> **Object** _____

> **Starts With The Letter _____**
>
> **Name** _____
> **Country** _____
> **Color** _____
> **Fruit/Vegetable** _____
> **Animal** _____
> **Job** _____
> **Verb** _____
> **Object** _____

> **Starts With The Letter _____**
>
> **Name** _____
> **Country** _____
> **Color** _____
> **Fruit/Vegetable** _____
> **Animal** _____
> **Job** _____
> **Verb** _____
> **Object** _____

> **Starts With The Letter _____**
>
> **Name** _____
> **Country** _____
> **Color** _____
> **Fruit/Vegetable** _____
> **Animal** _____
> **Job** _____
> **Verb** _____
> **Object** _____

Listen: The /l/ and /r/ sounds (2:16) Repeat after the speaker.

1. long wrong   4. collect correct   7. list wrist
2. play pray   5. pilot pirate   8. glass grass
3. light right   6. climb crime   9. fly fry

Circle the word that you hear the speaker say in the sentences below.

1. The (pilot / pirate) was in charge of the other men.
2. She taught us how to (play / pray).
3. Please put this on your (list / wrist).
4. Don't step on the (glass / grass).
5. The answer was (long / wrong).

Now take turns with a partner saying the sentences above. Choose a word to complete the sentence.

Lesson 12: A Horseman in the Sky

Look at the picture below. Discuss what you think the story will be about.

Biography and Background

Ambrose Bierce (1842-1913), American, was a reporter and novelist whose work was often tough and bitter. In **"A Horseman in the Sky,"** he writes of the U.S. Civil War in which the North — the Union — fights the South — the Confederate States. One major reason for this war was the issue of slavery. The state of Virginia at that time was on the dividing line, half North and half South. It symbolizes the tragedy of civil war anywhere, when brother fights brother, son fights father.

Listen: Comprehension (2:17) Listen to the story.

Option 1: Read along in your book.   **Option 2**: Listen to the story with your book closed.

A Horseman in the Sky

by Ambrose Bierce

It was a sunny afternoon in the fall of 1861. A Union soldier lay behind some bushes by a road on a cliff in western Virginia. He was sleeping, with his rifle lying beside him. If his commander knew he was sleeping at his post when he should be guarding the Union soldiers below, he would be punished by death. The road where the soldier was stationed was the only way out of the valley below. Down in that valley, the Union army was hiding. They were waiting for dark to climb the cliff and attack the enemy.

The sleeping soldier was a young Virginian named Carter Druse. He was the son of wealthy parents, whose home was only a few miles from where he was now. One morning he informed his father during breakfast that he wanted to join the war.

"Father, a Union army has arrived at Grafton. I am going to join it." His father looked at him, shocked, and after a moment of silence replied,

"Well, son, go and do whatever you feel is your duty. Virginia, to which you are a traitor, must get along without you. If we both live to the end of the war, we will speak about the matter some more." Carter walked away, nodding with respect, but with a broken heart.

He joined the Union army, and soon showed himself to be a brave and excellent soldier. But that afternoon, because of the terrible tiredness he felt, he fell asleep. Suddenly, he woke up, embarrassed that he had fallen asleep at his post. He quietly raised his head to look around to the cliff ahead. He saw the figure of a Confederate soldier on a horse against the sky. He was staring down into the valley. He must have seen the Union soldiers hidden among the trees. The gray uniform let Druse know that the man was the enemy. Completely awake, Druse brought his gun forward, and looked through the gunsight towards his new target.

At that instant the horseman turned his head and seemed to look into Druse's very face, into his eyes, into his brave heart. Druse became terrified at what he had to do. The enemy had seen him and knew the location of his company. Druse knew his duty: the enemy must be shot dead without any warning.

Many things went through his mind. Perhaps the enemy soldier saw nothing. Perhaps he was just admiring the beautiful landscape where Druse was hidden. Maybe the enemy soldier would simply ride away, back to where he came from. Then, in his mind came the words that his father had spoken to him before he left home.

"Whatever happens, do what you know to be your duty." His teeth were tightly closed, his breathing was slow and regular. He fixed his eyes, not on the man, but on the horse. Now! He fired. The man and the horse went riding straight and brave, down, down into the valley from the sky.

A few minutes later, an officer of the Union army slowly approached the young soldier from behind. Druse neither turned his head nor looked at him. He lay completely still.

"Did you fire?" the sergeant whispered.

"Yes."

"At what?"

"A horse. It was standing on the cliff over there, pretty far out. You see it is no longer there. It went over the cliff, down into the valley." Druse's face was white, but he showed no other sign of emotion. He turned away his eyes and said nothing more. The sergeant did not understand.

"That makes no sense, firing on a horse. I order you to report. Was there anyone on the horse?"

"Yes."

"Well?"

"My father was on the horse."

The sergeant rose to his feet and walked away. "My God!" he whispered to himself.

Vocabulary Find
Read through the story and circle any words or phrases that you don't understand. Discuss the words you circled and the vocabulary below with your teacher, or look them up in a dictionary.

soldier	duty	figure	warning
rifle	traitor	firing	company
post	uniform	target	sergeant

Expressions
Here are related expressions to the topic of the story: **DUTY**. Review as a class..

1. *"You can count on him."* (You can depend on him.)
2. *"Always let your conscience be your guide."* (Do what you know is right.)
3. *"He really dropped the ball on that one."* (He didn't do what he was supposed to do.)
4. *"She's just going through the motions."* (She doesn't really care about what she's doing.)
5. *"If you have a job, either big or small: Do it right or not at all."* (Do your best.)

Writing/Discussion
First, write short answers. Then discuss your answers in groups, or as a class.

1. Who were the main characters in the story? What do we know about them?

   _____

   _____

2. Why do you think Carter Druse wanted to fight in the war?

   _____

   _____

3. What went through Druse's mind when he saw the man on the horse?

   _____

   _____

4. Why was the sergeant so shocked at the end of the story?

   _____

   _____

5. What kinds of sacrifices are made during times of war?

   _____

   _____

Vocabulary Match
Match the vocabulary word to its definition. Work in pairs or as a class.

soldier   a place where a soldier stays and guards an area

rifle   to perform a responsibility correctly; requirement

post   a person who fights in a war

duty   a long and thin gun

traitor   a special kind of clothing worn to identify people belonging to a special group

uniform   someone who rebels or fights against his/her own people

figure   something to aim at (with a gun, perhaps)

target   form; shape

firing   a large group of soldiers in war

company   shooting a gun

sergeant   a soldier who is in charge of other soldiers

Let's Talk: Asking and Answering Questions

Your teacher will provide each student with a 3 x 5 card. On the card, each student will write down the name of a famous person, real or fictional, but preferably someone that everyone in the class would know. Students will each pin or tape their card to another student's back without their seeing it.

The students will walk around the classroom asking each other questions, trying to discover who he/she is. Some sample questions are placed below.

After everyone has guessed who he/she is, then change the cards to famous places, or things, or animals, and have the students go around asking questions again.

Am I from the United States?

Am I Tall?

Am I still alive?

Do I have blonde hair?

Do I play soccer?

Listen: Practice (2:18) Listen. Fill in the blanks below with the person describing himself/herself.

A basketball player

_____

A famous actress

_____

A company president

_____

A school teacher

_____

A famous writer

_____

A farmer

_____

Listen: The /ch/ and /sh/ sounds (2:19) Repeat after the speaker.

1. chips   ships
2. catch   cash
3. chin   shin

4. watching   washing
5. chops   shops
6. choose   shoes

7. cheat   sheet
8. chores   shores
9. witch   wish

Circle the word that you hear the speaker say in the sentences below.

1. I think I see some (chips / ships).
2. The people wanted to (catch / cash) some money.
3. He fell and hurt his (chin / shin).
4. She is (watching / washing) her car.
5. It was a story about three (witches / wishes).

Now take turns with a partner saying the sentences above. Choose a word to complete the sentence.

Lesson 13: Cinderella

Look at the picture below. Discuss what you think the story will be about.

Biography and Background

Grimm Brothers, Jacob (1785-1863) and **Wilhelm** (1786-1859), German, were more than brothers. They were close friends and worked together all their lives. They are best known for their collection of more than 200 oral fairy tales. These were old tales told by parents to children in many countries and in many, many languages around the world. **"Cinderella"** is this kind of story. *Grimms' Fairy Tales* has always been a favorite with children everywhere.

Listen: Comprehension (3:1) Listen to the story.

Option 1: Read along in your book. **Option 2**: Listen to the story with your book closed.

Cinderella

by the Grimm Brothers

Once upon a time, a long time ago and far away, there was a man who had a young, sweet and beautiful daughter. His wife died, and he married a second time. His new wife, now the girl's stepmother, was proud, rude, and mean. She had two daughters, as ugly as they were mean. The stepmother made the young daughter do all kinds of work around the house. She had to clean the dishes, sweep all the rooms, feed all the animals, and cook the meals. She gave her rags to wear. The other two daughters had beautiful clothes and lived a very easy life.

The poor father didn't know what to do because he was afraid of his new wife and stepdaughters.

When the girl finished all her work, she would sit by the fireplace and read. Her sisters began to call her Cinder-ella, or the girl who sits in the cinders of the fire. Soon everyone called her Cinderella.

One day, there came news that the prince of the land was going to hold a ball. The two sisters were invited. Cinderella had to sew their new dresses and iron all their clothes, as well as do all her other work. She wanted to go to the ball, too, but she knew that they would not allow her to go. When her stepmother and stepsisters left for the ball, Cinderella sat down by the fire and cried.

Suddenly a light appeared in the room, and then a beautiful woman stood before her.

"Who are you?" asked Cinderella.

"I'm your fairy godmother. I've come to help you prepare for the ball. You do want to go, don't you?"

"Oh, yes! More than anything. But I have nothing to wear, and no way to get to the castle."

"I will take care of that," said the fairy godmother. She took a pumpkin and touched it with her wand. It instantly became a fine carriage. She then touched her wand over six rats that were fighting over a small piece of bread. They instantly became fine horses to pull the carriage. She waved her wand over a small lizard that was passing by and it became the carriage driver.

"Oh, this is all so wonderful," said Cinderella. "But look at me, I cannot go in these rags. And there is no time for me to make new clothes." The fairy godmother touched her wand to Cinderella's clothes and instantly they became golden and silver cloth, with jewels sewn into the fabric. The dress was the most beautiful that Cinderella had ever seen, and on her feet were sparkling glass slippers.

"You must promise to come home before midnight," said the fairy godmother. "The magic will disappear after midnight. Remember."

"I'll remember," said Cinderella as she washed her face and did up her hair in beautiful fashion. She rushed off to the ball in her carriage. When she arrived, all the people were amazed at her beauty, and also by her elegant carriage.

"She must be a princess," someone said. Soon everyone was whispering about the unknown princess who suddenly appeared at the ball. Cinderella's stepmother and stepsisters did not even recognize her. The prince approached Cinderella and asked her to dance. He then asked her to sit next to him at the grand table. Cinderella was so happy. A great supper was served, and the prince talked to Cinderella the whole time. She found that she really liked the prince. But, oh, it was almost midnight! She apologized for leaving so soon. She did not want the prince to see her as she was before. As she was running out of the castle, she lost one of her glass slippers. She got home just before the carriage turned back into a pumpkin, and the dress turned back into rags.

The next day the prince found the glass slipper. He sent out a message for all the young ladies in the kingdom to try it on, so he could find the owner. A messenger brought the slipper to Cinderella's house. Her older sisters tried it on, but it would not fit. The messenger noticed Cinderella washing the floor in another room, and asked her to try it on.

"Oh, she isn't anyone important," said her stepmother. "She wasn't even at the ball." Still the messenger insisted that she try it on. It was a perfect fit. Suddenly, the fairy godmother appeared. She turned Cinderella's rags into beautiful clothing. They all realized that Cinderella was the beautiful princess they had all seen at the ball. The messenger rushed her back to the castle. Her stepmother and sisters begged Cinderella to forgive them. She did, with all her heart. She and the prince fell in love and soon married. Then, Cinderella and the prince lived happily ever after.

Vocabulary Find

Read through the story and circle any words or phrases that you don't understand. Discuss the words you circled and the vocabulary below with your teacher, or look them up in a dictionary.

insisted	stepmother	fireplace	iron
proud	stepdaughters	cinders	carriage
mean	ball	sew	glass slipper

Expressions

Here are related expressions to the topic of the story: **GOODNESS**. Review as a class.

1. *"She's a good (apple / egg)."* (She's a very nice person.)
2. *"He's about as good as they come."* (He is a really good person.)
3. *"She's an old friend of mine."* (She is a good friend from the past.)
4. *"She is a ray of sunshine."* (She is always happy and friendly.)
5. *"He has a heart of gold."* (He is a really good person.)

Writing/Discussion

First, write short answers. Then discuss your answers in groups, or as a class.

1. Who were the main characters in the story? What do we know about them?

_____

_____

2. What was Cinderella's life like after her father remarried?

_____

_____

3. Why couldn't Cinderella go to the ball?

_____

_____

4. What happened at the end of the story?

_____

_____

5. Do you think that nice people have good things happen to them? Why or why not?

_____

_____

_____

Group Answer

In groups of 4 or 5 complete the following activity.

Each group will take a turn sitting at the front of the class. Students will ask the group a question, and the group must answer the question together as quickly and accurately as possible. Each member of the group will add on to the word which was spoken by the person in front of him/her. After the group has answered three questions, switch groups.

Example: (Question) "Why are all of you sitting there at the front of the room?"

Answer: (Student 1) *"We...*   (Student 2) *are...*   (Student 3) *sitting...*   (Student 4) *here...*

(Student 1) *because...*   (Student 2) *our...*   (Student 3) *teacher...*   (Student 4) *is...*

Listen: Vocabulary Fill-in (3:2) First, choose and write the correct word in the sentences

below. Then listen to the speakers to check your answers.

1. She _____ on helping her mother clean the house.

   insisted   proud   mean   sew   iron   carriage

2. The girl was taken to the ball in a large _____ .

   insisted   proud   mean   sew   iron   carriage

3. The man was very _____ of the fact that he won the game.

   insisted   proud   mean   sew   iron   carriage

4. She had to _____ up the clothes that had torn.

   insisted   proud   mean   sew   iron   carriage

5. He wanted to _____ his shirt because it was badly wrinkled.

   insisted   proud   mean   sew   iron   carriage

6. The _____ stepsisters did not help her do the work.

   insisted   proud   mean   sew   iron   carriage

Let's Talk: Strange Behavior Read the instructions below and complete them as a class.

1. Look at some examples of the advice column in a local newspaper.

2. Divide into groups of two's or three's.

3. In groups, write a short letter asking for advice about what to do in a particular situation.

(The situations could include behaviors among the host country that are strange and confusing.)

4. Give the advice letters to the teacher to read aloud for the whole class to discuss.

5. Discuss what you would do, or what advice you would give.

Why do the people here...

...always speak so loudly?

...have three cars?

...date so many people?

...all have guns?

...watch so much television?

Listen: The /s/ and /sh/ sounds (3:3) Repeat after the speaker.

1. seat   sheet   4. sip   ship   7. sock   shock
2. save   shave   5. sew   show   8. massed   mashed
3. sell   shell   6. gas   gash   9. lease   leash

Circle the word that you hear the speaker say in the sentences below.

1. Do you have a (seat / sheet) for me?

2. He didn't (save / shave) it yet.

3. They took a (sip / ship) from the water.

4. It is a big (sock / shock).

5. The people were all (massed / mashed) together.

Now take turns with a partner saying the sentences above. Choose a word to complete the
sentence.

Lesson 14: A Chaparral Prince

Look at the picture below. Discuss what you think the story will be about.

Biography and Background

O. Henry's story, **"The Chaparral Prince"** takes place in about 1850 in the limestone quarrying area of Texas. Chaparral is a kind of low-growing bushy oak tree there. Many Germans lived and worked in towns nearby. The young girl, Lena, in this story, must have been reading **Grimms' Fairy Tales** in the original German. This is O. Henry's **"Cinderella"** story, with an unusual "prince" rescuing the girl.

A Chaparral Prince

By O. Henry

Lena was so tired. It was nine o'clock and she had been working all day long. She was eleven years old, thin, and hungry. Her whole body ached from all the work she had to do every day. She lit a candle in her room and sat down to write a letter to her mother.

Her father, who was mostly interested in money, sent her off to work in a rough hotel at the quarry. She missed her family, her friends, and her home. The only thing that comforted her was her book of Grimms' Fairy Tales. She read it every night before going to bed. She imagined that she was a princess locked up in an evil castle, and that a prince would come to her rescue. Grimms' stories helped her to escape from her misery, if only for a short moment. However, her boss, Mrs. Maloney, found her reading the other night and took the book from her. Now she was heart-broken. The only thing she could think of was to write a letter to her mother asking for help.

Lena's hometown in Fredericksburg, Texas, was where many Germans lived. It was 30 miles away from the quarry. Lena quickly wrote a letter to her mother, in her own German language. She dropped her letter out the window to a friend waiting below. Her friend delivered it to the local postman, Fritz Bergmann, telling him about the poor girl's terrible problems. Fritz promised to deliver the letter. That night, Fritz started out with his little mule wagon to deliver the mail to the people of Fredericksburg. Suddenly there appeared six men on horses, each one carrying a gun. They forced Fritz to stop and got off their horses.

"So, you're the postman. Throw down that bag of mail. Everyone knows that the Germans in Fredericksburg send money with their letters to each other." Fritz threw down the mail bag and the six robbers began opening the letters. They had opened up many, but did not find any money. One of the men started to rip open Lena's letter to her mother.

"Give me that letter," growled the leader of the robbers. "It's in German. Read it to us in plain English."

"Please be careful with that letter," cried Fritz. "That letter is from a poor little girl to her mother.

The girl is being worked to death at the hotel, and is begging to come home."

"How old is the girl?"

"Eleven."

"And she's working at the hotel? What is her father thinking?"

"Her father is very interested about money. I'm going to have a talk with him when I deliver the letter."

"You silly Germans, hiring out your children to be overworked, when they should be outside playing games and such..." The robbers found no money in any of the letters.

"Well, we've got to get going," said the leader. "We've got other places to rob. We're not going to hurt you, but we can't let you go around telling people about us, either." They tied Fritz, sitting against a tree, and got on their horses and left. He was all alone in the woods. He slept, and after several hours the robbers returned. They untied him.

"Go. Deliver your mail," said the leader. He gave a kick to the mules. Fritz went directly to Lena's house. He stopped at the gate and called. The family all rushed out. The mother asked him if he had a letter from Lena, and Fritz told them the whole adventure, including what he knew about poor Lena's problems. The father, when he heard the story, felt very sad for sending his daughter away.

"Oh, I was a fool to send her away. I hope that there is some way we can bring her back." Suddenly they heard a voice from the back of Fritz's wagon. There was an extra bag, and inside was little Lena.

"How did you get in there?" asked her mother.

"Last night, a young prince and his men came and rescued me from the hotel. They put me in the back of this wagon some place in the woods. It was cold, so I climbed into one of the bags and slept."

"Nonsense!" exclaimed her father. "Fairy tales! How did you really come from the hotel to the wagon?"

"The prince brought me," said Lena confidently. And to this day, the people of Fredericksburg haven't been able to make her give any other explanation.

Vocabulary Find Read through the story and circle any words or phrases that you don't understand.
Discuss the words you circled and the vocabulary below with your teacher, or look them up in a dictionary.

ached	fairy tales	misery	robbers
candle	castle	heart-broken	mules
quarry	rescue	postman	rip

Expressions Here are related expressions to the topic of the story: **DREAMS**. Review as a class.

1. *"You're dreaming if you think you can do that."* (It is too hard for you to do.)
2. *"The whole evening was a nightmare."* (The evening was terrible.)
3. *"The prince was an absolute dream."* (The prince was wonderful.)
4. *"Pinch me. I think I'm dreaming."* (I can't believe this is happening.)
5. *"Hey, wake up!"* (Pay attention to what you're doing!)

Writing/Discussion First, write short answers. Then discuss your answers in groups, or as a class.

1. Who were the main characters in the story? What do we know about them?

_____

_____

2. Why did the little girl write the letter?

_____

_____

3. What happened to the postman?

_____

_____

4. What happened to the little girl in the end?

_____

_____

5. Why do you think the robbers helped the girl?

_____

_____

Listen: Practice (3:5) Listen to the speakers as they spell their names. Write them below.

1. _____   6. _____

2. _____   7. _____

3. _____   8. _____

4. _____   9. _____

5. _____   10. _____

Let's Talk: Spell It Out
Work with a partner. Partner 1 look at Activity 14A on page 95. Partner 2 look at Activity 14B on page 96. Take turns spelling the words to each other. First, guess the word as you hear it. Then, write down the word in the blank below.

Word 1: _____   Word 10: _____

Word 2: _____   Word 11: _____

Word 3: _____   Word 12: _____

Word 4: _____   Word 13: _____

Word 5: _____   Word 14: _____

Word 6: _____   Word 15: _____

Word 7: _____   Word 16: _____

Word 8: _____   Word 17: _____

Word 9: _____   Word 18: _____

Vocabulary Match:
Match the vocabulary word to its definition. Work in pairs or as a class.

ache	a long stick of wax with a wick inside for burning to make light
candle	have very sore and stiff muscles
quarry	a place where rocks are cut from the ground
fairy tales	beautiful palace or home where a king and queen live
castle	stories about magic and princes and rescues
rescue	to have one's hopes destroyed suddenly
misery	save someone who is in danger
heart-broken	long-time suffering
postman	people who steal money or things from others
robbers	animals, like horses or donkeys, used to carry heavy objects
mules	a person who delivers the mail

Listen: The /s/ and /th/ sounds (3:6)
Repeat after the speaker.

1. sick   thick
2. sin   thin
3. pass   path
4. sink   think
5. mouse   mouth
6. sum   thumb
7. mass   math
8. sing   thing
9. suds   thuds

Circle the word that you hear the speaker say in the sentences below.

1. It looks a little (sick / thick)
2. They were looking for the (pass / path)
3. It's just a little (sin / thin)
4. They young man doesn't want to (sink / think)
5. It's a really big (sum / thumb)

Now take turns with a partner saying the sentences above. Choose a word to complete the sentence.

Lesson 15: The Griffin and the Minor Canon

Look at the picture below. Discuss what you think the story will be about.

Biography and Background

Frank R. Stockton (1834-1902) was an American journalist and writer of short stories for both children and adults. In this story, the Griffin is an imaginary flying monster that can be seen even today carved on some ancient churches of Europe. *"Minor"* here means not very important, and *"Canon"* means priest. Stockton's stories show great imagination, with fairy tale excitement and wonderful humor.

The Griffin and the Minor Canon

By Frank R. Stockton

Over the door of an old church in a quiet town there was a carved stone figure of an enormous griffin. The stone griffin had a large head, a huge open mouth and big, sharp teeth. Its back had great wings with sharp hooks. A long and powerful tail was at the end. It was truly an awful thing to look at. There were smaller copies of this stone figure along the sides of the church. The people were used to seeing them and paid no attention to them at all.

A long distance from the small town, and in the wilderness, lived the real Griffin. Somehow he found out about the stone statue. He had never seen what he looked like. There were no mirrors where he lived, and the river was too fast to see his reflection in it. He decided to visit the little church and see his image. He flew on and on, until he came to the countries where there were men. He finally landed outside a little town in a green meadow, where he rested after his long flight.

The news of his arrival spread quickly throughout the small town. The people were very scared and didn't know what to do. The Griffin stayed about half a mile outside the town. He called for someone to come and show him the stone statue, but no one dared to approach him. He saw two workmen hurrying home through the fields and ordered them to stop. The men stood trembling before him.

"What is the matter with you all? Isn't there anyone brave enough to speak to me?" asked the Griffin.

"I think," said one of the workmen, with his voice shaking, "that perhaps the Minor Canon would come." Whenever the people wanted something difficult done, such as visiting the poor and the sick, or teaching bad children in school, they always asked for help of the young priest, or Minor Canon, as he was called. The poor priest didn't want to be the one to talk to the Griffin, but he felt it was his duty to go.

"Well," said the Griffin, as the Minor Canon arrived. "I am glad to see that there is someone who has the courage to come and see me. I understand that there is a church in your town that has a stone statue that resembles me."

"Yes, that is correct." The priest looked at the frightening figure before him.

"I would like you to take me there. I would like to see it." The priest was very concerned about what the townspeople would do if he brought the Griffin to the church.

"It is getting dark now, and you won't be able to see the statue very well. If you would wait here until morning, I will come back and take you to the church."

"Agreed," said the Griffin. "I am tired and will take a nap here and cool my tail in this little stream. The end of my tail gets red hot when I am angry or excited, and it is quite hot now. I will see you tomorrow morning."

The Minor Canon was happy to leave, and raced back to town. He told the people about their conversation, and they were very nervous. Many began to discuss ways to rid themselves of the Griffin. Perhaps they could sneak up on it and kill it in the night. No one was brave enough to do it. What if they destroyed the statues on the church? The Griffin would have no reason to come into the town. But then he might become angry at the people for destroying the statue. In the end, they decided to leave it up to the Minor Canon.

The next morning, the Minor Canon went to meet the Griffin. It flew slowly through the air over his head, as they went through the silent city streets to the church. Not a person was to be seen. The Griffin looked up at the church where the Minor Canon pointed out the stone griffin. He was amazed at what he saw.

"Why, yes it must be me! How amazing." The Griffin continued to stare at the statue all morning and all afternoon. The priest became tired and hungry waiting with the Griffin.

"I'm going to go home and have supper. Would you like to join me?"

"No, I don't need to eat. I never eat between the equinoxes. At the next equinox I will eat a very good meal and it will last me for half a year. But if you need food, go ahead and leave me here. I know the way back to my resting spot."

The next morning the Griffin was found staring at the statue. This continued for days and days. The people in the town were very anxious. The Griffin was becoming very comfortable in the town, and began to look around at the school, at the shops and stores, and at the church meetings. He didn't seem to want to leave anytime soon. Many people left the town. Those who could not leave approached the Minor Canon and asked him how he was going to get rid of the Griffin. It spent so much time with him that the townspeople thought that he was the only one who could get rid of it...

Vocabulary Find
Read through the story and circle any words or phrases that you don't understand. Discuss the words you circled and the vocabulary below with your teacher, or look them up in a dictionary.

carved	awful	reflection	nap
equinox	mirror	priest	rid
hooks	meadow	raced	stare(ing)

Expressions
Here are related expressions to the topic of the story: **FEAR**. Review as a class.

1. *"He's afraid of his own shadow."* (He gets scared easily.)
2. *"I'm afraid I have to leave now."* (I'm sorry, but I have to leave now.)
3. *"You're really freaking me out, John."* (You're really frightening me, John.)
4. *"You scared the heck / devil out of me."* (You really scared me.)
5. *"He has nerves of steel."* (Nothing scares him.)

Writing/Discussion
First, write short answers. Then discuss your answers in groups, or as a class.

1. Who were the main characters in the story? What do we know about them?

_____

_____

2. Why did the Griffin go into the town?

_____

_____

3. What did the Griffin learn about the young priest?

_____

_____

4. What did the Griffin notice about the people?

_____

_____

5. How did the people treat the Griffin and the priest?

_____

_____

Listen: Practice (3:8)
Listen to the speakers. Write down what each person is afraid of.

1. _____ Steven
2. _____ Julie
3. _____ Kevin
4. _____ Susan
5. _____ Chad

6. _____ Rebecca
7. _____ John
8. _____ Cindy
9. _____ George
10. _____ Barbara

Listen: Vocabulary Fill-in (3:9) First, choose and write the correct word in the sentences below. Then listen to the speakers to check your answers.

1. The people wanted to get _____ of the Griffin from their community

    carved   **awful**   **reflection**   **priest**   **nap**   **rid**

2. The Griffin was an _____ creature to look at.

    carved   **awful**   **reflection**   **priest**   **nap**   **rid**

3. Because he was tired, he decided to take a short _____ .

    carved   **awful**   **reflection**   **priest**   **nap**   **rid**

4. The man could see his _____ in the mirror.

    carved   **awful**   **reflection**   **priest**   **nap**   **rid**

5. The young _____ was asked to take the Griffin out of the town.

    carved   **awful**   **reflection**   **priest**   **nap**   **rid**

6. The statue was _____ out of a large piece of rock.

    carved   **awful**   **reflection**   **priest**   **nap**   **rid**

Let's Talk: Overcoming Fears Discuss the following questions in small groups or as a class.

1. Do you feel afraid or embarrassed to speak English with native English speakers? Why or why not?

2. Were you afraid about coming to another country to live and study? Why or why not?

3. Does driving in a new country make you feel nervous? Why or why not?

4. Does the food in a new country make you afraid about gaining weight? Why or why not?

5. When was the last time you felt scared about something?

6. What did you do to overcome the fear you talked about in question #5?

7. What are the people in this country afraid of that you think is strange?

Listen: The /s/ and /z/ sounds (3:10) Repeat after the speaker.

1. ice   eyes   4. bus   buzz   7. sink   zinc

2. price   prize   5. peace   peas   8. miss   ms

3. sip   zip   6. racing   raising   9. once   ones

Circle the word that you hear the speaker say in the sentences below.

1. I have never seen (ice / eyes) like that before.

2. The (prices / prizes) looked very expensive.

3. Can you hear the (bus / buzz)?

4. Those (once / ones) looked very nice.

5. I am looking for (Miss / Ms.) Taylor.

Now take turns with a partner saying the sentences above. Choose a word to complete the sentence.

Lesson 16: The Griffin and the Minor Canon *(continued)*

Look at the picture below. Discuss what you think the story will be about.

He taught the lessons to the terrified children, who were the best behaved they had ever been.

The Griffin and the Minor Canon (continued)

By Frank R. Stockton

The people decided that the Minor Canon must go away into the wilderness so that the Griffin would follow him. The priest sadly agreed. The next morning the Griffin was still in the town. He seemed sorry that the priest was gone, but did not seem to care enough to look for him. Nobody was brave enough to tell the Griffin about their sending the Minor Canon off into the wilderness. So the Griffin stayed.

The Griffin had followed the Minor Canon so much, that he knew all about the priest's daily routine. He rang the school bell, calling all the kids to school. He taught the lessons to the terrified children, who were the best behaved they had ever been. He gave the church sermons. Everyone in town attended the meetings. The Griffin took care of the sick and the poor. Surprisingly, there were fewer sick and poor people with the visits of the Griffin. Nobody wanted to be sick or poor enough to have him come to their house.

The summer was passing very quickly. The Griffin kept busy doing all the things that the young priest used to do. The next equinox was quickly approaching and the townspeople were very worried. They were afraid that the Griffin would eat their children. They offered to cook him a great feast of anything he wanted. If he refused, they would tell him about an orphan asylum in the next town where he could eat the children. But he refused their offer.

"From what I have seen of the people of this town, I do not wish to eat anything that they prepare. They are all cowards and very selfish. And to even think about eating one of you is repulsive. The only person who could have satisfied my appetite was the Minor Canon, and he is gone away."

"Oh, it is too bad that we sent him away to the wilderness," said one of the old men of the town.

"What!" cried the Griffin. "You sent him away?" His tail began to turn red-hot and he began flying all over town, announcing to the people that he wanted everyone to meet him at the center of the town. In a few minutes the townspeople gathered around the Griffin.

"I am shocked at your selfishness. How could you be so cruel as to send that wonderful young priest out into the wilderness to starve to death. You are all very cruel. I know that you are afraid of me, but that is no excuse for what you have done. I shall go find him, if he is still alive, and will send him back to you. When he returns, you will treat him with the greatest respect or I will come back and destroy you all."

The Griffin left the town in search of the young priest. He found him in the wilderness, almost dead from hunger and thirst. The Griffin fed him some herbs and roots and fruits, and after a few days he became healthy again.

"Do you know that I like you very much?" asked the Griffin.

"I am very glad to hear it," said the Minor Canon.

"I'm not so sure you would be if you completely understood. If some things were different, other things would be otherwise. I was so angry at the people in your community that I ripped the stone statue off the top of the church. I will keep it here so that I never have to see them again. I will be content to look at my image when and for as long as I please. Lie down and have a good sleep, and then I will take you back to the town." When he was sound asleep, the Griffin took the Minor Canon back to the town and left him there.

The people of the town remembered the Griffin's threat. They happily greeted the priest and everyone attended his church sermons. The children were the best behaved kids ever. The Minor Canon was later appointed to the highest office of the old church. As the people were respecting him, they would often look up at the sky to see if the Griffin was coming. They learned to truly honor and respect the young priest, and not just because they were afraid of being punished.

But they had no reason to be afraid. The next equinox came and went, and there was no Griffin. The Griffin eventually died. It was a good thing that the townspeople did not know this. If you should ever visit the old town, you would still see the little griffins on the sides of the church; but the great stone griffin that was over the door is gone.

Vocabulary Find
Read through the story and circle any words or phrases that you don't understand. Discuss the words you circled and the vocabulary below with your teacher, or look them up in a dictionary.

wilderness	repulsive	feast	cruel
routine	appetite	coward(s)	herb(s)
behaved	equinox	selfish	threat

Expressions
Here are related expressions to the topic of the story: **CHANGE**. Review as a class.

1. *"He turned over a new leaf."* (He made some changes in his life.)
2. *"He made a 180 degree turn."* (He changed his life completely.)
3. *"Now he's heading in the right direction."* (Now he's doing what he should be doing.)
4. *"Some things never change."* (Disappointment at not having any change.)
5. *"You need to turn your life around."* (You need to make changes in your life.)

Writing/Discussion
First, write short answers. Then discuss your answers in groups, or as a class.

1. What did the Griffin do when the priest left the town?

_____

_____

2. How did the people react to the Griffin?

_____

_____

3. Why did the Griffin become so angry?

_____

_____

4. Why did the people change their attitude toward the priest?

_____

_____

5. What can be learned from this story?

_____

_____

_____

Listen: Practice (3:12)
Listen. Match the speakers to the changes they would like to make in life.

1. Stephanie   would like to exercise more often.
2. James   wants to change jobs and do something more challenging.
3. Barbara   would like to spend more time with the family.
4. Greg   wants to learn how to cook better meals.
5. Wendy   would like to learn how to swim.
6. David   wants to work less and go out more often with friends.
7. Kathy   would like to read more often.

Vocabulary Match Match the vocabulary word to its definition. Work in pairs or as a class.

wilderness   an action that is done over and over again

routine   something disgusting; sickening

repulsive   the forest, or desert that is far away from the city and people

appetite   hunger

feast   people who are afraid; not brave

cowards   a big meal with very special food

selfish   mean, unkind

cruel   wanting only to satisfy oneself, thinking only of oneself

herbs   promising punishment if something is not done

threat   plants that can be used to heal, or to eat

Let's Talk: Changes In groups, or as a class, discuss the following questions about culture shock.

1. Describe three things that surprised you when you arrived in this country.

2. Was it hard to adjust to life here? Explain.

3. What is culture shock?

4. Does everyone go through culture shock when they live in a different place?

5. What are three things that you would change about the new country if you could?

6. What advice would you give to people going through culture shock?

7. Would it be hard for you to return home after living abroad?

8. If you could live anywhere in the world, where would it be?

Listen: The /d/ and /the/ sounds (3:13) Repeat after the speaker.

1. day	they	4. Dan	than	7. breed	breathe
2. dare	their	5. dough	though	8. d's	these
3. doze	those	6. Dave	they've	9. riding	writhing

Circle the word that you hear the speaker say in the sentences below.

1. (Day / They) came at about 7:00 a.m.

2. I don't want (D's / these) for my grades.

3. (Dave / they've) already brought some food.

4. Are you making (dares / theirs)?

5. Are those animals in the zoo (breeding / breathing)?

Now take turns with a partner saying the sentences above. Choose a word to complete the sentence.

Lesson 17: The Locket

Look at the picture below. Discuss what you think the story will be about.

Biography and Background

Kate Chopin (1851-1904) was a novelist and short story writer. She was known for modernist and feminist writings of her time. Her short stories, like **"The Locket,"** were called by some critics as being "among the few unquestioned masterpieces of American short story art."

Listen: Comprehension (3:14) Listen to the story.

Option 1: Read along in your book.   **Option 2**: Listen to the story with your book closed.

The Locket

by Kate Chopin

One warm evening a few soldiers were gathered around a fire. They were waiting for orders to enter battle the next morning. Two soldiers were lying down, relaxing. A third man lay back in the shadows, not joining the conversation. The fourth was intently reading a letter. He opened his collar and shirt.

"What's that you've got around your neck, Ed?" asked one of the men. Ed ignored the question and continued reading his letter.

"Is it your sweetheart's picture?" continued the man. "Maybe it's just a lucky charm that keeps you from getting hurt. So far you haven't received even a small scratch." Ed looked up from his letter and smiled.

"It must be a lucky charm, Nick. I don't think I could have gone through this year and a half without it." The letter had made Ed heart sick and home sick. He opened up the locket and looked at the picture of his beautiful Octavie, who had given it to him. It had both their names on it. Inside he had placed a small piece of paper with his name, his hometown, and a message to please return it to Octavie if anything happened to him. It was his most precious possession. He fell asleep thinking about Octavie and their future, if he lived through this terrible war. But he dreamed of a serpent around his throat. He tried to grab it, then it was gone.

"Get your stuff, Ed! We're going, right now!" shouted Nick. Ed woke up startled, and quickly gathered his things together. As they got ready, each soldier wondered if this fight would be his last.

The battle was fierce. The smoke cleared and the troops withdrew. All that remained in the field were bodies of fallen soldiers. A priest walked among them.

He searched for survivors, but there were no signs of life anywhere. Other priests looked among the dead for personal belongings to be sent back to family members. There was a soldier—only a boy—lying with his face to the sky. One of this hands held a locket tied around his neck. The priest gently removed it and searched for other identification. He found none. Inside the locket he found the note.

It had been about a week since she received the letter and the locket. Octavie was very sure that she would never be happy again. She and her family went to the small church to mourn the man who was to become her husband. All that remained of her sweetheart was the locket. There was no way to bring the body home. It was most likely buried at some battle site in an unmarked grave.

"I shall die an unmarried, unhappy woman," she whispered to herself. She looked at the locket, and then at family and friends who had gathered for the funeral. Among them was a dear and familiar face. As she approached, she couldn't believe her eyes. She ran to the man and hugged him tightly.

"It must have been stolen from me the night before the battle," he said. "In the confusion the next day I didn't realize that my locket was gone. I thought I had lost it during the battle."

"Stolen?" she asked. She thought of the dead soldier who was wearing the locket when it was found. Ed said nothing, but he was remembering his fellow soldier, the one who had stayed back in the shadows—the one who had not joined the conversation.

Vocabulary Find: Read through the story and circle any words or phrases that you don't understand. Discuss the words you circled and the vocabulary below with your teacher, or look them up in a dictionary.

soldiers	collar	locket	fierce
battle	sweetheart	hometown	troops
shadows	lucky charm	serpent	mourn

Expressions Here are related expressions to the story topic: **FEELINGS**. Review as a class.

1. *"The woman was feeling a little blue during work."* (She was feeling sad.)
2. *"He said that he was feeling kind of up and down."* (He was feeling good and bad.)
3. *"Robert was feeling down in the dumps."* (Robert was feeling sad.)
4. *"She's as happy as a clam."* (She is very happy.)
5. *"The news really caught me off my guard."* (I was shocked /surprised by the news.)

Writing/Discussion First, write short answers. Then discuss your answers in groups, or as a class.

1. Who is the main character in the story and what do we know about him?

   _____

   _____

2. Why does Ed have a locket?

   _____

   _____

3. What happens to Ed during the battle?

   _____

   _____

4. How does the war affect Octavie?

   _____

   _____

5. What happens to Ed and Octavie in the end?

   _____

   _____

Let's Talk: How Are You? Work with a partner. Look at the pictures below and on the next page. Take turns explaining how the people are probably feeling and explain why.

Listen: Practice (3:15) Listen to the situations. Circle how the speaker is feeling.

Person 1:	happy	sad	angry	embarrassed	nervous	jealous	frustrated	scared
Person 2:	happy	sad	angry	embarrassed	nervous	jealous	frustrated	scared
Person 3:	happy	sad	angry	embarrassed	nervous	jealous	frustrated	scared
Person 4:	happy	sad	angry	embarrassed	nervous	jealous	frustrated	scared
Person 5:	happy	sad	angry	embarrassed	nervous	jealous	frustrated	scared
Person 6:	happy	sad	angry	embarrassed	nervous	jealous	frustrated	scared
Person 7:	happy	sad	angry	embarrassed	nervous	jealous	frustrated	scared
Person 8:	happy	sad	angry	embarrassed	nervous	jealous	frustrated	scared

Listen: The /ch/ and /j/ sounds (3:16) Repeat after the speaker.

1. cheer   jeer
2. chain   Jane
3. age   H
4. choking   joking
5. chunk   junk
6. chill   Jill
7. cherry   Jerry
8. chin   gin
9. search   surge

Circle the word that you hear the speaker say in the sentences below.

1. The crowd was (cheering / jeering) when the team scored.
2. I think those are (chains / Jane's), aren't they?
3. You forgot your (H / age) on this application.
4. I thought that the man was (choking / joking).
5. Those are (cherries / Jerry's), I think.

Now take turns with a partner saying the sentences above. Choose a word to complete the sentence.

LESSON 17: The Locket   **69**

Lesson 18: To Build a Fire

Look at the picture below. Discuss what you think the story will be about.

Biography and Background

Jack London (1876-1916), American, wrote about big cities and small towns, but his real fame was for writings about man against nature. **"To Build a Fire"** takes place in the Yukon area of Alaska. People living there know that temperatures often go 50 degrees below zero, and that fingers and toes can freeze solid in 2 or 3 minutes if not protected. His characters are often foolishly brave.

Listen: Comprehension (3:17) Listen to the story.

Option 1: Read along in your book.   **Option 2**: Listen to the story with your book closed.

To Build a Fire

By Jack London

The day was terribly cold and gray. The young man had taken a new snow-covered path, trying to arrive at the camp by six o'clock. His buddies would be waiting for him there, with a good dinner and a warm fire. This part of the Yukon trail was unfamiliar to him. But he could make it before night came.

He continued to walk along, glad that he carried very few things. He only brought food for lunch with him. He thought about the warm fireplace, but it made his hands and feet seem colder. He walked a little faster. With him was his dog, a big gray husky. The young man noticed that even the dog seemed cold, and wanted a place out of the wind. He rubbed his cheeks and nose with the back of his hand, but they were numb. He had never known such cold.

It was about ten o'clock, and he was traveling about four miles an hour. At half past twelve he arrived at a creek he knew. There he stopped to eat lunch. It was at least 10 miles to camp, and it would probably take him three more hours, at least. He ate his meal and then started walking again. After another hour, he realized that he was really cold, especially his hands and his feet. If he was not careful, his fingers and toes could freeze, and he would really be in trouble. He decided to stop and build a fire to warm his frozen boots, gloves and also his body. He found some small branches and bits of wood. He cleared away the snow under a tree, away from the wind. He took out a match and carefully lit it. He finally had a small flame going. He was very careful to add small branches, then larger ones, not wanting to kill the fire. The fire must not go out, or he could easily freeze to death before getting another one started. The fire began to grow larger. Soon he would have warmth all over his body. Then after his gloves and boots were unfrozen, he could continue. He felt safe with the fire glowing in front of him. He took off his gloves and placed them near the fire. He then tried to remove his boots. It was painful when the warmth hit his fingers and toes, they were so cold and numb. After a few minutes the pain went away and the warmth began to sink in.

Then it happened. The tree where the man had built the fire was heavily loaded with snow. When he broke off a dead branch, a huge mass of snow came down and put the fire out. He was shocked. Suddenly there was no fire, no warmth, and no safety. After staring at the spot for several minutes in disbelief, he realized that he was in danger. Another fire had to be started. This time, it could not go out.

He had no time to put on gloves or boots. His fingers were so numb he could barely control them. He could not feel his feet anymore, and it was difficult to walk. Yet he continued to work as quickly as he could. He brought out his box of matches, but they fell to the ground. He tried to pick them up and put them back in the box, but his fingers didn't work. He finally managed to pick them up and remove one to start the fire. He put the match in his mouth and tried to strike it against a flat rock. It lit, but the smoke made him sneeze, and it went out. Desperately he took the whole box between the palms of his hands and somehow struck a match inside. All of the matches began to burn inside the box. The man knew that his palms were burning, yet he felt nothing. He held the burning box to the bits of wood, trying desperately to light them. He dropped the box, hoping that it would be enough to get a fire started, but it fell too far away, and the fire went out.

Now panic began to set in. He looked at his dog. Perhaps he could use it for warmth. He called to the dog. It must have sensed the man's fear, and it ran away. He struggled to put on his frozen boots and gloves. Maybe he could still make it to the camp. He felt panic, and began running. He ran up the trail with the dog just behind him. He ran with a fear he had never known in his life. It was the certain fear of death. It was not just that his hands and feet were frozen, but it was a matter of life and death. He finally stumbled and fell. He must sit and rest.

Now he began to feel comfortable, almost warm. Yet, when he touched his nose and cheeks, there was no feeling. He was losing his fight with the icy cold. He became calm, and very sleepy. A good idea, he thought, to sleep off to death. A great peace of mind came over him. He closed his eyes. There were many worse ways to die.

The dog howled for a few moments, then turned and trotted up the trail to the camp it knew...

Vocabulary Find
Read through the story and circle any words or phrases that you don't understand. Discuss the words you circled and the vocabulary below with your teacher, or look them up in a dictionary.

unfamiliar	creek	numb	strike
husky	meal	glowing	lit
rubbed	gloves	shocked	desperately

Expressions
Here are related expressions to the topic of the story: **WEATHER**. Review as a class.

1. *"It's really coming down right now."* (It is really raining or snowing hard.)
2. *"He said he was freezing to death."* (He said he was terribly cold.)
3. *"It looks clear right now."* (No clouds are in the sky.)
4. *"It's really pouring right now."* (It is really raining hard.)
5. *"I think the storm will blow over."* (The storm will not bring rain or snow.)

Writing/Discussion
First, write short answers. Then discuss your answers in groups, or as a class.

1. Who is the main character and what do we know about him?

   _____

   _____

2. Why is the man outside all alone?

   _____

   _____

3. After he starts the fire, what happens?

   _____

   _____

4. Why can't the man start another fire?

   _____

   _____

5. How does the story end?

   _____

   _____

Listen: Practice (3:18)
Listen to the weather forecast. Fill in the blanks with the words you hear.

Today we should see mostly _____ skies. Light _____ are forecast

for this afternoon. The high for today is expected to be around _____ degrees.

The low for tonight should be around _____ degrees. Tomorrow there is a

_____ % chance of _____ in the afternoon and a chance of

_____ in the mountains. Scattered rain _____ are likely tomorrow

night, with snow falling in the _____. Highs tomorrow should be in the upper

_____ and lows should be in the lower _____. Currently we

have a temperature of _____ degrees under mostly _____ skies.

Listen: Vocabulary Fill-in (3:19) First, choose and write the correct word in the sentences below. Then listen to the speakers to check your answers.

1. Because of the extreme cold, the man's fingers were _____ and he couldn't feel them.
   unfamiliar   rubbed   creek   numb   shocked   lit

2. The people were _____ with the city and didn't know where they were going.
   unfamiliar   rubbed   creek   numb   shocked   lit

3. The two men went fishing at a small _____ in the mountains.
   unfamiliar   rubbed   creek   numb   shocked   lit

4. She _____ a match to start the fire.
   unfamiliar   rubbed   creek   numb   shocked   lit

5. The people were _____ when they heard the news.
   unfamiliar   rubbed   creek   numb   shocked   lit

6. The man _____ his hands together to try to get them warm.
   unfamiliar   rubbed   creek   numb   shocked   lit

Let's Talk: Weather Work in small groups. Respond to the following questions.

1. Which type of weather would you be able to tolerate more: really hot or really cold? Explain.

2. Would you prefer to walk outside if it is snowing or raining? Explain.

3. How do you like the weather where you are now?

4. Do you have seasons where you live? What are they like?

5. What was the worst weather experience you have ever had?

6. Does the weather have any influence on how you feel?

7. What would be the perfect day (weather) for you? Explain.

8. What would be the worst day (weather) for you? Explain.

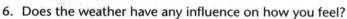

Listen: The /k/ and /g/ sounds (3:20) Repeat after the speaker.

1. class	glass	4.	back	bag	7.	docks	dogs
2. coat	goat	5.	cold	gold	8.	cuts	guts
3. clue	glue	6.	lock	log	9.	curls	girls

Circle the word that you hear the speaker say in the sentences below.

1. She has a lot of (cuts / guts), doesn't she?

2. This is a large (class / glass), isn't it?

3. That is a very large (coat / goat).

4. The (clue / glue) is sitting right over there.

5. It looks like it may be (cold / gold).

Now take turns with a partner saying the sentences above. Choose a word to complete the sentence.

Lesson 19: The Tell-Tale Heart

Look at the picture below. Discuss what you think the story will be about.

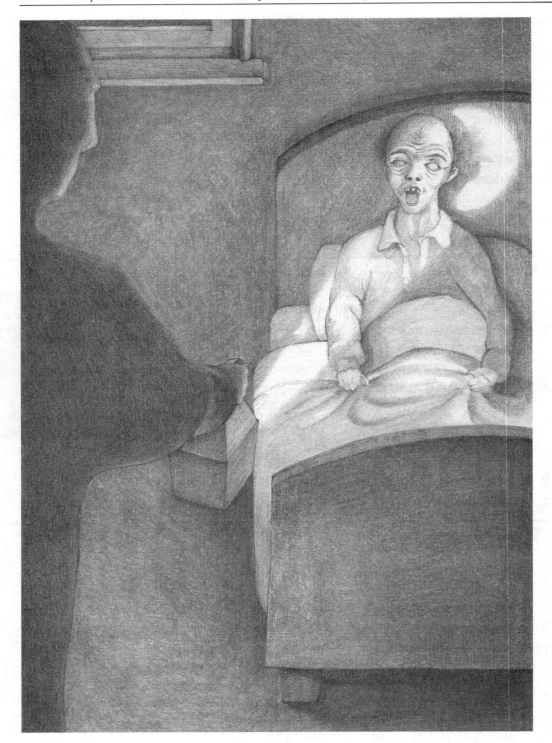

Biography and Background

Edgar Allan Poe (1809-1849) Poe was an American journalist, poet and short story writer. Although he had great success with his writing, Poe's family life was unhappy. He married his cousin, age 13, who died a few years later. Tragedy seemed to follow him. He suffered from depression and madness, and struggled with drinking and drugs. He was a master of horror stories, such as **"The Tell-Tale Heart,"** and **"Murders in the Rue Morgue,"** thought of as the basis of our modern detective story.

The Tell-Tale Heart

By Edgar Allan Poe

It is true, I was very, very nervous. But why do you think that I have gone mad? Listen carefully as I tell you the entire story, then you may decide for yourselves whether or not I am truly a mad man!

It is hard to say how the idea first entered my mind, but once it did it haunted me day and night. Strangely enough, I loved the old man. He had never wronged me the entire time I worked for him. I did not do it for money. I did not do it for revenge. I think it was the old man's eye! Yes, it was that evil eye, one that stared pale blue with a white film over it. Whenever he looked at me with that eye my blood ran cold. I decided that I must take the life of the old man and rid myself of the eye forever.

I know that you surely think me a mad man. But mad men are ignorant and stupid. I was very wise in the way I proceeded. I was very cautious, very careful and creative. I was never kinder to the old man than in the few weeks before I killed him. Every night I would carefully open his bedroom door and peek inside. Now would a mad man have been so clever?

For several nights I opened the door and looked inside. I wanted to see the evil eye, but each night I entered, it was closed. With the eye closed, there was no need for action. Each morning I would enter the room confidently and try to cheer the old man's spirits. I inquired how he had slept, and he never once realized that someone was spying on him during his sleep.

One evening I looked in and was about to open the light in my lantern. My thumb slipped and the fastening made a loud noise. The old man sprang up in the bed, crying out, "Who's there?" I kept still and said nothing. For a whole hour I did not move a muscle. He had not laid back in bed, yet. I heard a slight groan and I knew the man was terrified. He must have been trying to calm himself down, but it did him no good this night. Tonight he must have felt that death was stalking him.

When I had patiently waited a very long time, I opened the lantern a tiny bit until a single ray fell upon his evil eye. It was open, wide open, and I became furious as I looked at it. It was time to take action. As I crept quietly towards the bed, I heard a noise. It was the beating of the old man's heart. It made me even more obsessed with destroying him. Louder and louder the sound of the beating heart grew. I could no longer wait. Someone would surely hear the low thudding of the old man's heart!

With a loud yell I leaped upon the old man. He screamed only once. I dragged the bedding over the top of him. Slowly the sound of the beating heart decreased, until finally I could no longer hear it. His eye would trouble me no more.

If you still think I am a mad man, you will no longer think this way when I describe how careful I was to hide the old man's body. I took up three boards from the floor and placed the body inside. After I replaced the boards, there was no way that anyone would know about the murder. There was no blood to wash out, no stain of any kind. I had been too clever for that.

It was about 4:00 in the morning when I finished. Suddenly I heard someone knocking at the door. I went downstairs and opened it. Three men introduced themselves as police officers. A neighbor had heard a scream and called the police to come and investigate.

I smiled. What had I to fear? I asked the gentlemen to come inside and make themselves comfortable. The scream, I told them, was my own. I had a bad dream during the night. I took the visitors all through the house and let them search wherever they wished. When we returned to the main room, I placed my own chair over the very spot where the old man lay.

The police officers were satisfied. I had convinced them. I was completely calm and they suspected nothing. But after a few minutes, I grew tired of their presence and wished that they would leave. In the back of my mind I heard a low dull sound. I became pale and nervous. The sound was not coming from within, but from outside. I talked more quickly, with more feeling, and yet the officers stayed. I got up and paced around the room, but yet the dull beating sound continued to get louder and louder. And still the officers chatted pleasantly, and smiled. Did they not hear the pounding sounds? Was it possible? No.

They knew, they suspected, but they were making me suffer. Anything was better than this agony. Anything was better than watching them smile at me and know about the beating getting louder and louder!

"Villains!" I screamed, "I admit the deed! Tear up the floor! Here, here is the beating of his hideous heart!'

Vocabulary Find: Read through the story and circle any words or phrases that you don't understand. Discuss the words you circled and the vocabulary below with your teacher, or look them up in a dictionary.

clever	revenge	investigate	beat(ing)
rid	ray	groan	obsessed
haunted	spying	lantern	hideous

Expressions Here are related expressions to the topic of the story: MADNESS. Review as a class.

1. *"It's driving me nuts."* (It really bothers me.)
2. *"He's a little bit of a fruit cake, if you ask me."* (He seems strange to me.)
3. *"Have you lost your mind?"* (Are you serious about doing this?)
4. *"She has a screw loose, or something."* (Very strange/weird/nuts.)
5. *"That guy is psycho!"* (That man is crazy.)

Writing/Discussion First, write short answers. Then discuss your answers in groups, or as a class.

1. Who are the two main characters in the story and what do we know about them?

_____

_____

2. Why does the servant want to kill the old man?

_____

_____

3. Why does the servant insist that he is not mad (crazy)?

_____

_____

4. How do the police discover the man's crime?

_____

_____

5. How does the story end?

_____

_____

_____

Listen: Practice (4:2) Listen to the speakers. Write down what makes each person go crazy. (upset)

1. Lewis _____

2. Rachel _____

3. Dean _____

4. Angela _____

5. Mark _____

6. Lisa _____

Vocabulary Match Match the vocabulary word to its definition. Work in pairs or as a class.

clever   a small line of light

revenge   smart, intelligent

ray   wanting to punish another for what he/she did to you

spying   secretly watching

groan   an object that will carry a flame inside for light

lantern   a low sound made when someone is afraid or in pain

obsessed   to hit

beat   thinking about something all the time

rid (of)   to make something leave or be gone

Let's Talk: It Drives Me Crazy Discuss in small groups what you would do in each situation:

1. You are trying to study, but the people living next door have their music turned up loud and it is distracting you.

2. You are watching a movie, but there are some people sitting behind you talking and laughing all the time. It's hard for you to watch the movie.

3. You and your friends decide to go out to a restaurant. It is so full that you will have to wait an hour before you can be seated. Your friends want to stay anyway.

4. A construction crew is working on the road that you take to work. At 8:00 and at 5:00 the traffic is terrible.

5. You and your friends are waiting in a long line to get tickets to an event. It is freezing cold outside and you have another six hours before tickets go on sale.

6. You want to improve your English ability by speaking in English as much as possible. Your friends continue to talk to you in your native language.

Listen: The /w/ and /v/ sounds (4:3) Repeat after the speaker.

1. whale   veil   4. wheel   veal   7. wiser   visor

2. wine   vine   5. west   vest   8. went   vent

3. worse   verse   6. wow   vow   9. wiper   viper

Circle the word that you hear the speaker say in the sentences below.

1. I have never seen a (whale / veil) like that.

2. That (wheel / veal) doesn't look very good.

3. The (West / vest) is very pretty.

4. The (wines / vines) are in good condition.

5. Her message is a little (worse / verse).

Now take turns with a partner saying the sentences above. Choose a word to complete the sentence.

Lesson 20: The Cow-Tail Switch

Look at the picture below. Discuss what you think the story will be about.

Biography and Background

Jabo may be a person, or possibly a tribe of Africa. It is hard to know where this story comes from. In Nigeria alone there are more than 450 languages spoken. This is likely an oral tale, as are most African stories of the past. They continue even today. Such tales are meant to entertain, to teach right from wrong, to keep knowledge alive, to fight illness and death, and to support the society's culture. **"The Cow Tail Switch"** is a fine example.

Listen: Comprehension (4:4) Listen to the story.

Option 1: Read along in your book.   **Option 2**: Listen to the story with your book closed.

The Cow-Tail Switch

By the Jabo

A hunter by the name of Ogaloussa lived in the village of Kundi. One morning he took his weapons and went into the forest to hunt. The day and the night passed and he did not return. Another day and night passed and still he did not return. His family talked about it and wondered what had happened to him. A week passed, then a month. The family took care of the small farm and the sons hunted for animals. After a month, they no longer talked about Ogaloussa's disappearance.

Then one day, another son was born to Ogaloussa's wife. His name was Puli. Puli grew older and began to sit up and crawl. When Puli spoke, the first words he said were, "Where is my father?"

The other sons looked out into the forest. "Yes," one of them said. "Where is father?"

"He should have returned a long time ago," said another.

"Something must have happened to him. We should go look for him."

"I saw the direction he traveled. I can help us find him."

So the sons took their weapons and went into the forest to find Ogaloussa. When they were deep inside the forest, they found an old trail and followed it. As they came to a place where the trees had died, they found the bones of their father. He had been killed while he hunted. One of the son's stepped forward. "I know how to put a dead person's bones together." He gathered all of Ogaloussa's bones and put them together.

Another son said, "I know how to cover the bones with muscles and skin." He went to work and he covered the bones with muscles and skin.

A third son said, "I know how to put blood into a dead body." He went forward and put blood back into Ogaloussa's body.

Another son said, "I can put breath into a dead body." He worked until they saw Ogaloussa's chest rise and fall.

"I can give him the power of movement," another son said. He put the power of movement into Ogaloussa's body and he began to sit up. Then he stood up and looked at them.

"I can give him the power of speech," said another son. He gave Ogaloussa the power to speak and then they all stood back. Ogaloussa looked at them.

"Where are my weapons?" he asked. The sons picked up the weapons and gave them to him. They all returned home. When Ogaloussa arrived home his wife prepared a bath for him, gave him much to eat, and prepared a bed for him to rest. After five days Ogaloussa finally left his house. He had shaved his head because this is what people did after they came back from the land of the dead.

He prepared a great feast to celebrate his return from the dead. Before the feast, he took a cow's tail and braided it. Then he decorated it with beads and shells and bits of shiny metal. It was a beautiful thing, and many men in the village wanted it. Ogaloussa informed them that he would be giving it to one of his sons at the celebration.

During the celebration Ogaloussa stood up and spoke. "A long time ago I went into the forest to hunt. While I was hunting, a leopard attacked and killed me. Then my sons came for me. They brought me back from the land of the dead. I will give this cow tail to one of my sons. I have only one cow tail to give. I shall give it to the one who did the most to bring me home."

One of the sons said, "He will give it to me. I put his bones together."

"No, he will give it to me," said another. "I put his muscle and skin together."

"No, he will give it to me," said another. "I gave him power and movement." The sons all argued amongst themselves about who would receive the cow tail. Ogaloussa quieted his sons and spoke.

"To this son I will give the cow-tail switch, for I owe him the most." He came forward and handed it to Puli, the little boy who had been born while Ogaloussa was in the forest. The sons and the people of the village knew that he was right because the child's first words were, "Where is my father?" For it was a saying among them that a man is not really dead until he is forgotten.

Vocabulary Find

Read through the story and circle any words or phrases that you don't understand. Discuss the words you circled and the vocabulary below with your teacher, or look them up in a dictionary.

weapons	forest	muscles	breath
disappearance	trail	skin	speech
crawl	bones	blood	shaved

Expressions

Here are related expressions to the topic of the story: **LOYALTY**. Review as a class.

1. *"He's true blue."* (He's very loyal and dependable.)
2. *"You can count on him."* (He is dependable.)
3. *"She won't let you down."* (You can depend on her.)
4. *"I owe you one."* (I will repay you the favor.)
5. *"The man was a real go-getter."* (The man was enthusiastic and worked hard.)

Writing/Discussion

First, write short answers. Then discuss your answers in groups, or as a class.

1. Who are the main characters in the story and what do we know about them?

_____

_____

2. What happens to Ogaloussa?

_____

_____

3. What do the sons do to bring Ogaloussa back to life?

_____

_____

4. What happens at the celebration?

_____

_____

5. What can be learned from the story?

_____

_____

Listen: Practice (4:5)

Listen to the speaker. Fill in the clocks with the times you hear.

1. _____ 2. _____ 3. _____ 4. _____ 5. _____ 6. _____

Listen: Vocabulary Fill-in (4:6) First, choose and write the correct word in the sentences below. Then listen to the speakers to check your answers.

1. The men picked up their _____ and prepared for the battle.

   weapons   crawl   forest   trail   bones   muscles

2. Many people want to improve their bodies by exercising their _____.

   weapons   crawl   forest   trail   bones   muscles

3. Babies learn to _____ before they can walk.

   weapons   crawl   forest   trail   bones   muscles

4. The people wanted to take a hike through the beautiful _____.

   weapons   crawl   forest   trail   bones   muscles

5. The people found some old _____ buried in the sand.

   weapons   crawl   forest   trail   bones   muscles

6. The man followed the _____ out of the jungle.

   weapons   crawl   forest   trail   bones   muscles

Let's Talk: Telling Time Practice saying the time with a partner. There may be more way than one to state the time. Ask your teacher about the different ways to say the time.

10:05	1:30	4:25	7:15	8:30	12:00
3:20	5:35	6:10	11:25	2:20	4:55
6:45	10:18	7:57	12:02	1:47	3:33
5:50	11:09	3:41	6:19	12:42	4:01

Listen: Intonation (4:7) Listen to the following information about intonation.

In English, intonation is used to show emotion, add emphasis on words, or clarify information. Listen to the different situations that have similar intonation patterns.

Statements

My name is David.	She is a friend of mine.	He wants to come.
I played football yesterday.	She went to the party.	He typed on the computer.

"WH" Questions

Where are you going?	When are you leaving?	Which one do you want?
Why did you do that?	What do you want?	Who is that man?

YES / NO Questions

Did you see the accident?	Are you going to the party?	Is he your best friend?
Was he in your class?	Do you like to play baseball?	Have you been here before?

Lesson 21: A Self-Made Man

Look at the picture below. Discuss what you think the story will be about.

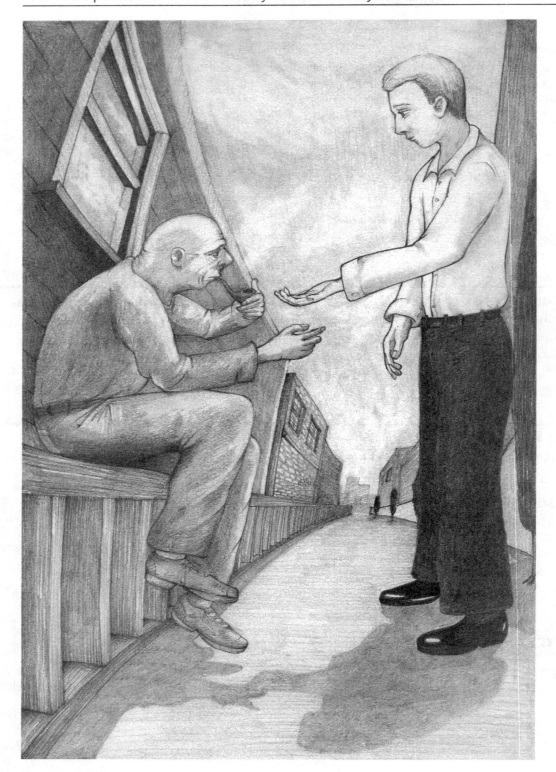

Biography and Background

Stephen Crane (1871-1900) an American journalist and short story writer who believed in the importance of chance and freedom of choice in life. He valued individual responsibility. The character in **"A Self Made Man"** shows great self-confidence as he creates the environment that helps him become successful.

Listen: Comprehension (4:8) Listen to the story.

Option 1: Read along in your book.   **Option 2**: Listen to the story with your book closed.

A Self-Made Man

By Stephen Crane

Tom had a hole in his shoe which was very round and uncomfortable. He used up almost two packs of playing cards by putting them inside his shoe four at a time. The cards wore out, so he had to replace them daily. One day Tom was walking down Broadway looking for work. He owed money for his room, but his nice landlady had confidence in him. She trusted him because he was very confident and sure of himself. So he strolled along the street looking for opportunity to come his way.

Suddenly he saw an old man sitting upon a railing, smoking a pipe. Tom stopped to look because he wasn't in a hurry, and it was an unusual sight. He wanted to investigate a little bit. He walked up to the old man, who seemed to be in deep thought.

"Got a match?" Tom inquired. The old man looked surprised at Tom. Then he leaned forward and looked deeply in Tom's eyes.

"Son, can you read?" he asked.

"Yes, I can read." He no longer had any interest in a match. The old man fumbled in his pocket and took out a paper.

"You look honest, son. I've been looking for an honest fellow for almost a week. I've been sitting on this railing for six days waiting." He handed a letter to Tom.

"Read it for me, son." Tom took the letter and began reading.

Office of Ketchum R. Jones, Attorney at Law, Tin Can, Nevada

Rufus Wilkins

Dear Sir, I have not yet heard from you about the sale of your land, which I explained to you in a letter on June 25. I request an immediate reply concerning it. I have sold the three corner lots at five thousand dollars each. Please give me your address and your attorney's address, and I will send the papers and then the money. Please respond right away...

"Yes," cried the old man. "I've heard enough. It is just as I thought. My son George is trying to rob his own father. Tears slowly trickled down his face.

"Come now," said Tom, patting him on the back. "What you should do is get a lawyer and go visit George."

"Tell me where to get one, and I will," replied the old man.

"Well, I could be your lawyer," said Tom.

"You, a lawyer?"

"Well, I could pretend to be your lawyer and your son wouldn't know I'm not. And it wouldn't cost you a cent."

"Come on then," replied the old man. "Let's go visit George." They left the street and soon arrived at the son's house. George was working busily at his desk when they entered the room.

"George," said the old man in a loud voice. "This is Mr. Smith, my lawyer. We want to know what you did with the letter that was sent on June 25th." George was so surprised that he spilled his coffee.

"What do you mean, Father?" replied George very feebly.

"What I mean is give me the paper or my lawyer will take care of it for me." George looked at Tom, who was pretending to be businesslike and professional.

"Well, I suppose I could give you the money that was sent," replied George very quietly. He reached into his wallet and handed the money to the old man. On their way out of the room, Tom looked back and glared at George, making him shrink back into his chair.

"Oh, how you took care of him!" said the old man. "And now I'm going to take care of you." The old man sent Tom money every month, and Tom became quite a good businessman. After a while he was well respected in the city, and many people looked up to him as a role model to follow. A newspaper asked him about his success. He said, "To succeed in life, when you see an old man sitting upon a railing, smoking a pipe, go up to him and ask him for a match."

Vocabulary Find

Read through the story and circle any words or phrases that you don't understand. Discuss the words you circled and the vocabulary below with your teacher, or look them up in a dictionary.

opportunity	railing	attorney	shrink
packs of cards	pipe	lot(s)	respected
landlady	match	glared	model

Expressions

Here are related expressions to the story topic: **INTELLIGENCE**. Review as a class.

1. *"He's pretty sharp."* (He's very smart.)
2. *"She's a very bright girl."* (She is intelligent.)
3. *"John has a good head on his shoulders."* (John is a smart person.)
4. *"This decision is a no-brainer."* (This decision is easy to make.)
5. *"The test was a piece of cake for Susan."* (The test was very easy for Susan.)

Writing/Discussion

First, write short answers. Then discuss your answers in groups, or as a class.

1. Who are the two main characters in the story and what do we know about them?

   _____

   _____

2. Why did the young man stop to ask for a match?

   _____

   _____

3. Why has the old man been waiting?

   _____

   _____

4. How does Tom help the old man?

   _____

   _____

5. How does the story end?

   _____

   _____

Listen: Practice (4:9)

Listen. Write down what each person is studying in college.

1. Tom _____
2. Terry _____
3. Holly _____
4. Wayne _____
5. Sally _____

6. Jamie _____
7. Greg _____
8. Nicole _____
9. Brian _____
10. Amanda _____

Vocabulary Match
Match the vocabulary word to its definition. Work in pairs or as a class.

landlady	an object that can be used for smoking tobacco
pipe	a person who manages an apartment or house
match	someone who understands the law and works for others; lawyer
attorney	a small piece of wood or cardboard hit against a rough surface to make fire
shrink	well-liked by others, admired
respected	to become smaller or less significant
railing	pieces of land
lots	someone that others wish to follow or be like
model	metal pieces or wood used for support on stairs; fence

Let's Talk: Intelligence and Teamwork Work in teams of two or three.

Your teacher will have the following materials for each team.

1. 25 index cards per team
2. Masking tape
3. Scissors (optional)

Turn to page 95 for instructions for the activity.

Listen: Word endings (4:10) Listen to the speakers say the following words. Repeat after the speakers. Circle the ending that is used.

-es ending					**-ed ending**			
apples	/s/	/z/	/uz/		grabbed	/d/	/t/	/ud/
loses	/s/	/z/	/uz/		cracked	/d/	/t/	/ud/
boxes	/s/	/z/	/uz/		hurried	/d/	/t/	/ud/
tents	/s/	/z/	/uz/		laughed	/d/	/t/	/ud/
maps	/s/	/z/	/uz/		spied	/d/	/t/	/ud/
pens	/s/	/z/	/uz/		smacked	/d/	/t/	/ud/
pies	/s/	/z/	/uz/		hunted	/d/	/t/	/ud/
laughs	/s/	/z/	/uz/		mopped	/d/	/t/	/ud/

Listen to the speakers say the following sentences. Circle the word you hear.

1. My friend (can / can't) go with us.
2. I (can / can't) drive a truck.
3. She (can / can't) speak Japanese.
4. (Can / Can't) you help me?
5. She (can / can't) talk right now.
6. The secretary (can / can't) help you.
7. My brother (can / can't) sing very well.
8. We (can / can't) go to the movie tonight.
9. I (can / can't) come tonight.
10. (Can / Can't) you come?
11. He (can / can't) play the violin.
12. (Can / Can't) you dance very well?
13. We (can / can't) study here right now.
14. Our baby (can / can't) talk.
15. I (can / can't) see it from here.

Now take turns with a partner saying the sentences above. Choose a word to complete the sentence.

Lesson 22: The Invalid's Story

Look at the picture below. Discuss what you think the story will be about.

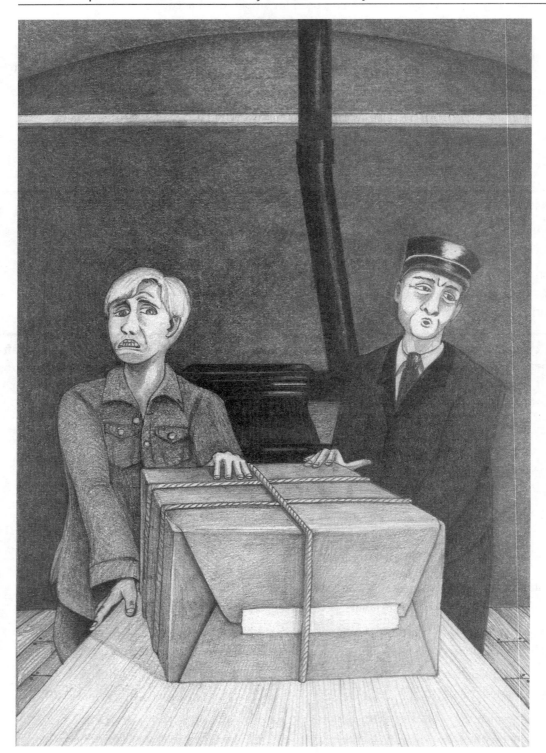

Biography and Background

Mark Twain is the name used by Samuel Clemens (1835-1910), American journalist, novelist and short story writer of great good humor. He is remembered especially for **The Adventures of Tom Sawyer** and **Huckleberry Finn**. In **"The Invalid's Story,"** the invalid (sick man) begins his story with two great, funny sentences that let us readers know we are about to hear a wonderful, though unbelievable tale.

Listen: Comprehension (4:11) Listen to the story.

Option 1: Read along in your book.   Option 2: Listen to the story with your book closed.

The Invalid's Story

by Mark Twain

I appear sixty and married, but this is because of my sufferings. I am actually single and only forty-one. Just two years ago I was a strong, hearty man. Now I am weak and tired all the time. The way I lost my health is very strange, indeed. I lost my health by taking a box of guns on a two hundred mile railway journey one winter's night. It is the truth. Here is my story.

I lived in Cleveland, Ohio. One winter's night two years ago I arrived home to find out that one of my dear friends, John B. Hackett, had died the day before. His last wish was that I take his body home to his poor father and mother in Wisconsin. I agreed.

When I arrived at the train station, I found a long white-pine box waiting for me. I wrote a card with my name, as owner of the box, where it was going, and saw it carried into the express car. I then went to the eating room to get myself a sandwich. When I returned I saw a young man stapling a card to a long white box. I rushed to the express car and there I saw the box with my card on it. (The fact is that a terrible mistake had been made. I had a box of guns the young fellow was shipping, and he had my corpse.)

I jumped into the express-car with the box of guns, which I thought was my poor dead friend, and the train left the station. The expressman of the train greeted me. He was a nice man who worked hard. As we were moving faster along the track, a stranger entered the car and set down a package at one end of my coffin box—I mean my box of guns—and left. I found out later that the package contained Limburger cheese. Now I know about the terrible stench that Limburger cheese can produce. But at the time, it was just another package to us.

The expressman made a big fire in the stove and the room became warmer. Slowly the odor of the cheese reached our nostrils. We tried to ignore the smell, which we thought was coming from my dead friend, but it was no use. It was very noticeable. The expressman walked over to the box of guns and took in a sniff, then came back and sat down by me.

"Was he a friend of yours?"

"Yes," I replied.

"He's pretty smelly, isn't he?" We both sat there quietly for a few moments, not knowing what to say to each other. The expressman broke the silence.

"What did he die of?" I replied that I didn't know.

"How long has he been dead?"

"Two or three days." We both stared at the box, wondering what the dead body must have looked like. The smell continued to get worse.

"I've carried many dead bodies on this train before, but this one has to be the very worst." It was clear to us that something had to be done. The smell was becoming intolerable.

"What if we give the box a shove toward the other end of the car? Maybe the smell wouldn't be so bad here near the stove." I agreed that it was worth a try, and we both tried to move the box with the rifles. The expressman slipped and fell near the box of cheese and he gasped for air. He ran to the door and opened it up to get some fresh air. We wanted to keep the door and window open, but it was so cold that we would freeze.

"Well, it looks like he's going to stay right where he is," stated the expressman. "He's going to have his way with us. We'll have to think of something else." He went to a cupboard and took out a bottle of liquid used for cleaning. It was carbolic acid. He began to sprinkle it all over the box and over the package of cheese. Soon the two smells combined and we both had to run to the door again for air. By the time we closed the door we were almost frozen. We sat very close to the stove for warmth, struggling with the terrible odor that filled the car.

"Yep, it looks like your friend is going to have his way. It doesn't look like there's much we can do," said the expressman. "There may be one last chance, though." He gathered up some chicken feathers, dried apples, tobacco, old shoes, and some other things and piled them up on the floor and set fire to them. Now the original smell had the smell of things burning. We had to head for the door again.

"It looks like your friend wants to travel alone," commented the expressman. "Our only choice is to sit out in the cold and let him be alone." About an hour later, we were taken from the platform. We were both frozen and almost dead. It was a few hours later that we were informed that we had spent the night with a harmless box of rifles and a lot of smelly cheese. The news was too late to save me. My health has been permanently altered and I will never be the same again.

Vocabulary Find
Read through the story and circle any words or phrases that you don't understand. Discuss the words you circled and the vocabulary below with your teacher, or look them up in a dictionary.

hearty	coffin	stench	intolerable
stapling	expressman	odor	carbolic acid
claimed	Limburger cheese	nostrils	platform

Expressions
Here are related expressions to the story topic: **MISFORTUNE**. Review as a class.

1. *"We're up the creek (without a paddle)."* (We are in trouble. We have problems.)
2. *"I'm at the end of my rope."* (I don't think I can continue like this.)
3. *"It was a tough break for the baseball team."* (The baseball team had bad luck.)
4. *"He really did a number on me!"* (He really got me / caused problems.)
5. *"Well, that's the way the ball bounces."* (Sometimes things don't go very well.)

Writing/Discussion
First, write short answers. Then discuss your answers in groups, or as a class.

1. Who are the main characters in the story and what do we know about them?

2. Why is the man on the train? Where is he going?

3. Why does the train car smell so bad?

4. What do the men try to do to stop the smell?

5. What do the men discover at the end of the story?

Listen: Practice (4:12)
Listen. Circle if the person's experience was lucky or unlucky.

1. **Peter**   Lucky   Unlucky
2. **David**   Lucky   Unlucky
3. **Sarah**   Lucky   Unlucky
4. **Katy**   Lucky   Unlucky
5. **Nathan**   Lucky   Unlucky
6. **Rachel**   Lucky   Unlucky
7. **Brent**   Lucky   Unlucky
8. **Paula**   Lucky   Unlucky
9. **Daniel**   Lucky   Unlucky
10. **Amy**   Lucky   Unlucky

Listen: Vocabulary Fill-in (4:13) First, choose and write the correct word in the sentences below. Then listen to the speakers to check your answers.

1. The person who had died was placed in a wooden _____ .

   claimed   coffin   stench   nostrils   intolerable   platform

2. The man _____ the box to be his.

   claimed   coffin   stench   nostrils   intolerable   platform

3. The people stood on the _____ waiting for the train.

   claimed   coffin   stench   nostrils   intolerable   platform

4. The smell was _____ and the people walked out of the room.

   claimed   coffin   stench   nostrils   intolerable   platform

5. There was a terrible _____ that came from the old house.

   claimed   coffin   stench   nostrils   intolerable   platform

6. The two men breathed in the bad-smelling air with their _____ .

   claimed   coffin   stench   nostrils   intolerable   platform

Let's Talk: Lucky Guess Work in teams of three. Listen as your teacher reads you a riddle. (pg. 97) Work as a team to try to figure out the riddle. See which teams can get the most riddles correct.

Listen: Word stress (4:14) Listen to the information below about word stress.

All words in English are made up of syllables. Look at the words with one syllable.

book   pen   keys   walk   speak

Look at the words with two syllables. Notice that one syllable is spoken with more strength than the other syllable. This is called word stress.

pa per   **ri** ver   com **plete**   **mor** ning   **wea** ther

Listen to the following words. They have been divided into syllables. Put a stress mark (') above the syllable that you hear being stressed. The first one has been done for you.

| yes' ter day | a no ther | chil dren | ba na na | a gain |
| for get | help ful | com pa ny | va ca tion | tel e phone |

Look at the words below. A stress mark has been placed on the stressed syllable. Practice saying the words with your teacher.

to day'	pro' blem	im por' tant	vi' si tor	base' ball
prac' tice	a bove'	el e va' tor	dri' vers	com pu' ter
lo ca' tion	tea' cher	class' room	stu' dent	friend' ly

Lesson 23: The Revolt of Mother

Look at the picture below. Discuss what you think the story will be about.

Biography and Background

Mary Wilkins Freeman (1852-1930) was an American poet and writer of short stories. She grew up in a farming town in Massachusetts during hard times. Her stories were called "too realistic" for a woman writer. Women were not supposed to be independent. In the story **"The Revolt of Mother"** she shows the husband (Father) as a truly good man who finally realizes that he has not been fair to his family.

The Revolt of Mother

by Mary Wilkins Freeman

"Father, why are those men digging in the field?" Sarah Penn looked at her husband, Adoniram. It appeared that he didn't hear her, as he was busy taking the saddle off his horse.

'I know you can hear me, Adoniram. Why are those men digging over there in the field?"

"They're digging a cellar."

"A cellar for what?"

"A barn."

"A barn? You're building another barn over there where we were going to build a new house?"

"I ain't got nothing to say about it. I wish you'd go into the house and do your work." He led the horse into the old barn. His wife of more than thirty years stood there staring at him. Her son, Sammy joined her as she watched the men busily working in the field.

"Is your father going to buy more cows for the new barn?"

"I think he said he was going to buy four more cows." His mother did not say anything. She just stood there looking at the men working in the field. It was her dream to have a new house. The old house was too small and it was falling apart. She had often spoken to her husband about building a new house. For over thirty years he promised her a new home when they had the money. One day as Adoniram returned from working on the barn, she was waiting for him.

"We finally have the money to build a new house, Father."

"I ain't got nothing to say about it," was his reply.

"Look at this house," she said as they both walked inside. "Look at the unfinished stairs that go up to the small bedrooms. Look at this kitchen. It's terrible in here. I've never complained to you about anything in thirty years. But now I have to tell you I want a new house. Our daughter Nanny's going to be married soon. How can she have a wedding in this terrible living room? You're willing to spend money on a new barn for the animals, while we live in a place like this. It doesn't make sense."

"I ain't got nothing to say about it," was the only thing he said.

The barn was completed after three weeks of work. Friends in the neighborhood came to admire the new barn. Adoniram was very pleased. Sarah did not speak of it any more.

"It's strange how your mother feels about the new barn," said Adoniram to Sammy one day. Sammy knew he should not answer his father.

Adoniram prepared his horse. He was going on a three day trip to bring four cows back to the new barn. Sarah said goodbye and watched him as he rode away. She stared at the barn for a long time. The workmen were busy gathering hay and preparing to put it in the new barn.

"Stop!" she shouted to the men. "Don't put the hay in that barn. Put it in the old barn."

"But Adoniram said to put it in here," one of the workmen replied.

"Yes, but I'm telling you to put it in the old barn." As the men were putting the hay in the old barn, Sarah stared at the new barn and began to smile.

"Sammy, go get your sister. I need you two to help me with something."

Adoniram returned with four new cows. He tied up the cows and went to the house. The door was locked. He went around to the back and found it locked up as well. Confused, he walked over to the new barn. "What's that smell?" he said to himself. "It smells like cooking. But that's impossible!" He opened the door and looked inside. There was his wife cooking at a stove. All the furniture was inside and the children were busy helping their mother.

"What's going on?" he gasped.

"You'd better take off your coat. Supper will be ready in a few minutes." She continued cooking, not noticing that her husband stood still, just staring at her. Finally he spoke.

"I don't understand, Sarah." She continued cooking and after a few minutes turned to set the table.

"I've waited thirty years for a new house, and I've finally got one. Of course, you'll have to set up some walls for the bedrooms, and make some new windows on one side, but I think it will be just fine."

"But what about the cows and what have you done with the other animals?"

"They're in the house. It will be just fine for the animals. Please come and sit down. Supper's ready."

Adoniram ate without speaking during supper. Afterward, he went out and sat down on the step by the door. He leaned his head on his hands. Sarah went out to him. She bent over him. He was weeping.

"Father, please don't cry."

Adoniram spoke softly. "I'll fix it up pretty for you, Mother. I had no idea how much you wanted a new house."

Vocabulary Find
Read through the story and circle any words or phrases that you don't understand. Discuss the words you circled and the vocabulary below with your teacher, or look them up in a dictionary.

cellar	wedding	stove	leaned
barn	hay	furniture	bent over
stairs	neighborhood	gasped	weeping

Expressions
Here are related expressions to the story topic: **DETERMINATION**. Review as a class.

1. *"You just have to hang in there."* (Don't give up / Keep going.)
2. *"She is always aiming for the sky."* (She is always trying her best.)
3. *"Jack is always fired up."* (Jack is determined to succeed.)
4. *"The people decided they would never give in."* (The people will do their best.)
5. *"You need to keep your eye on the prize."* (You need to work hard to have success.)

Writing/Discussion
First, write short answers. Then discuss your answers in groups, or as a class.

1. Who are the main characters in the story and what do we know about them?

   _____

   _____

2. Why is Sarah surprised that her husband is building a barn?

   _____

   _____

3. What does Sarah do while her husband is gone away buying the cows?

   _____

   _____

4. Why is Adoniram surprised when he gets home?

   _____

   _____

5. Have you ever been as determined to do something as Sarah? Explain.

   _____

   _____

Listen: Practice (4:16)
Listen. Write down what each person's future plans are.

1. _____   6. _____
2. _____   7. _____
3. _____   8. _____
4. _____   9. _____
5. _____   10. _____

Vocabulary Match Match the vocabulary word to its definition. Work in pairs or as a class.

cellar	a place where animals and farming equipment are kept
barn	an appliance used to cook food
hay	a place underneath the house; similar to basement
stove	similar to grass; used as food for animals
furniture	to show shock or fear; breathe in hard from surprise
gasp	couch, chairs, sofa, table, etc.
leaned	crying; showing sadness
weep(ing)	rested on something: bent downward

Let's Talk: The Future Discuss the questions below in groups or as a class.

1. What do you plan to do after this course is finished?
2. Do you plan to travel to any other countries? Explain.
3. Would you be interested in learning another language? Why or why not?
4. Do you have any big goals that you want to accomplish? What are they?
5. How will you use English in the future?

Listen: Reductions and Linking (4:17) Listen to the speakers say the following sentences. Notice how the italicized words are reduced when they are spoken.

1. I *have to* leave at 3:00.   (have to > /hafta/)

2. Susan *has to* call her husband.   (has to > /hasta/)

3. We *had to* leave the party.   (had to > /hadda/)

4. We've *got to* help them.   (got to > /gotta/)

5. He *ought to* buy these shoes.   (ought to > /otta/)

6. They *want to* go to that store.   (want to > /wanna/ or /wanta/)

7. Steven is *going to* call me.   (going to > /gonna/)

8. I *used to* live there.   (used to > /usta/)

9. They *don't know* what to do.   (don't know > /donno/)

10. We *don't want to* do that.   (don't want to > /dowanna/)

11. Can you *give me* some money?   (give me > /gimme/)

12. *Let me* help you with that.   (let me > /lemme/)

13. *Come on* over at 10:00.   (come on > /kmon/)

14. *Nothing* happened at school.   (nothing > /nothin/)

15. *Did you* see the accident?   (did you > /didja/)

Appendix 1: Additional Activities

Lesson 14A Let's Talk: Spell It Out
Spell the following words to your partner. Don't let him/her write anything as you spell the word. Have your partner write the word only after he/she correctly guesses the word.

1. c-l-a-s-s-r-o-o-m
2. c-h-a-i-r
3. s-t-u-d-e-n-t
4. c-a-l-c-u-l-a-t-o-r
5. p-a-p-e-r
6. t-e-a-c-h-e-r
7. l-a-n-g-u-a-g-e
8. f-r-i-e-n-d-s-h-i-p
9. b-l-a-c-k-b-o-a-r-d
10. c-o-m-p-u-t-e-r
11. b-u-i-l-d-i-n-g
12. a-n-i-m-a-l
13. w-a-t-e-r-f-a-l-l
14. a-p-p-l-e
15. b-e-a-u-t-i-f-u-l
16. J-a-n-u-a-r-y
17. s-t-o-m-a-c-h
18. h-e-l-p-f-u-l

Lesson 21: Intelligence and Teamwork Activity
In this activity you will work together with some index cards, tape, and scissors (optional). Your objective is to compete against the other teams to gain as many points as possible. In order to receive points, your team must build a small building (paper house) that is better than the others. You start out with 300 points.

A. You will have **5 minutes** to study the instructions as a team, and decide how you will make your building. Think about how many points to spend. Think about how many points you will earn!

B. In order to use the materials to build your building, you must buy them from your teacher.

    1 card = 10 points (maximum of 25 cards)

    1 inch of tape = 1 point (no maximum)

    scissors = 25 points (optional)

C. You will have **20 minutes** to build your building.

D. You will receive points for the following things.

    1. finishing on time = **100 points** For each minute you are late, you will lose 10 points.

    2. floor and roof = **50 points**   If your building has a floor and roof, you will receive 50 points.

    3. size = **1 point** per square inch   (L x W) Multiply the length and width for total area.

    4. beauty = **100 points**   100 points for the most beautiful, 75 for second, 50 for third.

    5. stability = **150 points**   50 points if it stays together when dropped from 6 feet. 100 points if it stays together when a small book is dropped on it

Remember: You want to earn the most points in order to win.

Lesson 14B Let's Talk: Spell It Out
Spell the following words to your partner. Don't let him/her write anything as you spell the word. Have your partner write the word only after he/she correctly guesses the word.

1. b-l-a-n-k-e-t
2. k-i-t-c-h-e-n
3. D-e-c-e-m-b-e-r
4. g-r-a-s-s
5. i-n-s-t-r-u-c-t-o-r
6. t-a-b-l-e
7. s-c-h-o-o-l
8. b-r-e-a-k-f-a-s-t
9. a-u-t-o-m-o-b-i-l-e

10. s-p-e-l-l-i-n-g
11. W-e-d-n-e-s-d-a-y
12. c-h-i-c-k-e-n
13. s-t-u-d-y-i-n-g
14. a-n-g-r-y
15. m-o-t-h-e-r
16. b-r-a-i-n
17. t-e-l-e-v-i-s-i-o-n
18. s-u-n-l-i-g-h-t

Lesson 22: Lucky Guess
The teacher will read the following riddles to the students. Students can take notes while they listen. The first group to correctly answer the riddle will receive a point. See which group gets the most points.

(Answers can be found on page 107)

Riddle #1   Two U.S. coins equal 30 cents. One is not a quarter. What are the two coins?

Riddle #2   A man walked into a pet shop and bought a parrot. The parrot was guaranteed to repeat everything it heard. However, the parrot never said a word. The owner took it back complaining, but was told that the guarantee was not broken. Why not?

Riddle #3   I am an only child, but the child of that man is my father's son. Who is it I am referring to?

Riddle #4   A plane crashed on the border of Canada and the United States. Where should the survivors be buried?

Riddle #5   Two women and their daughters are eating in a restaurant. Only three people are at the table. How is this possible?

Riddle #6   Suppose that you are driving from Philadelphia to Boston at a speed of 90 miles per hour (mph). At the same time, your friend is driving from Boston to Philadelphia at a speed of 60 mph. When the two cars meet, who is closer to Boston?

Riddle #7   Two brothers were born on the same day, at the same time, in the same year, and at the same hospital. They have the same mother and father, but they are not twins. How are they related to each other?

Riddle #8   A ship has a ladder on one side. There are 25 inches between each step. Ten steps of the ladder are under water at high tide and twenty steps are above water. If the water level goes down 75 inches at low tide, how many steps will be outside the water?

Riddle #9   A spider is at the bottom of a 30 meter hole. The spider is trying to climb out. It climbs up 4 meters in daylight, but at night it becomes confused and climbs down three meters. At this rate, how long will it take the spider to crawl out?

Riddle #10   A man is driving in his car when he sees an automobile accident. He stops to help because he is a doctor. He is very upset when he discovers that the injured person is his son. He takes his son to the hospital as quickly as possible. When the boy is taken into surgery, another doctor enters, looks at the boy, and says, "I can't operate on this boy. He's my son!" How is this possible?

Appendix 2: Tapescript / Answers

Lesson 1

Listen: Practice (1:2) Listen to the short stories. Put them in order as you hear them from 1 to 5. Discuss whether you think each story is true or not true and why.

1. One day during the winter I went grocery shopping. When I came back out I couldn't find my car keys. I searched my purse and my pockets, but couldn't find them. I went into the store, but they weren't there, either. On my way out, I just happened to look over into the snow, and I saw something. When I went over and looked closer, it was my keys! I couldn't believe that I lost them in the snow, but it was even harder to believe that I found them again.

2. I went swimming at this lake near my house. Somehow I got out too far and was starting to get really tired. I shouted for help, but there wasn't anyone around. As I was going under the water, I felt something grab me and bring me back up to the surface. It was my dog, Sam. He then helped me make it back to shore. If it hadn't been for Sam, I probably would have drowned.

3. One day I was cleaning the house, when I accidentally got some cleaning liquid in my eyes. I knew that I needed to see a doctor because rinsing them out with water only made them hurt even more. I got in my car and managed to drive to the hospital, even though I couldn't see very much in front of me. It's incredible that I was able to drive that far without being able to see.

4. I was fishing out on a lake, when my boat suddenly started sinking. I did everything I could to stay afloat, but the boat finally sank. I didn't have my life jacket with me, which was stupid, but I stayed afloat out there in the middle of the lake for about two hours before someone came and rescued me.

5. My friends and I were jumping off my roof into the swimming pool below. I know it was a stupid idea, but it was a lot of fun at the time. One of my friends was about to jump, when he slipped. We could tell that he wasn't going to make it to the pool, but fortunately he fell into some bushes instead of hitting the ground. He was all scratched up, but he wasn't hurt. We all stopped jumping off the roof after that.

    <u> 5 </u>   A. This story is about a group of boys who went swimming and almost had an accident.
    <u> 1 </u>   B. This story is about a woman who lost and found her car keys.
    <u> 3 </u>   C. This story is about a young girl who drove a car from her house to the hospital.
    <u> 4 </u>   D. This story is about an old man who survived a boating accident.
    <u> 2 </u>   E. This story is about a young boy who was saved by his dog.

Listen: Vocabulary Fill-in (1:3) First, choose and write the correct word in the sentences below. Then listen to the speakers to check your answers.

1. It was a real **tragedy** when the young boys were hurt in an accident.
2. He had a very **creepy** feeling as he walked inside the old house.
3. The little boy was very **mischievous**. He always got into things and made a mess.
4. The young woman was very **mature** for her age. It was hard to believe she was only 15.
5. The party was **lively**. Everyone was dancing and playing games and having fun.
6. The men walked around in the **swamps** until their boots were full of mud and water.
7. It was really cold and all the boys **shivered** as they went outside.
8. The woman's **niece** talked to the guests while she was preparing dinner.

Lesson 2

Listen: Practice (1:6) Listen to the people as they describe embarrassing things that happened to them. Match the person to the embarrassing situation.

1. I was playing baseball with my kids in the back yard one day. My son was having a hard time hitting the ball, so I decided to show him how to do it. I had him throw me the ball and I hit it, but I hit it too hard and it went over the fence and broke our neighbor's window. I was really embarrassed when I went over to explain what had happened.

2. I was talking with one of my teachers after class and I was calling him Professor Johnson. After a few minutes he informed me that he was not Professor Johnson, but Professor Jenkins. I was so embarrassed. I had forgotten his name and was using another professor's name instead.

3. My friends all say that I have a nice singing voice and want me to sing at parties and other events. I hate my voice and I really feel awkward singing in front of others.

4. I had to call the police to come open my car for me. I accidentally left my keys in the car. It was in a busy parking lot and everyone was watching as about four policemen tried to get it open. I was so embarrassed.

5. I was having lunch with a friend of mine and we were talking. I reached for the sugar and spilled my coffee all over the table and all over my dress. I stood up and kind of screamed a little bit because it was hot. Everyone started looking at me and I was so embarrassed.

1.	D	William	A. person spilled coffee all over his/her clothes in a restaurant
2.	C	Robert	B. person locked his/her keys in his car
3.	E	Sally	C. person forgot his/her professor's name
4.	B	James	D. person accidentally broke his/her neighbor's window
5.	A	Mary	E. person gets embarrassed when he/she is asked to sing in public

Listen: Practice (1:7) Now listen to the six situations from the previous page and write down what the person does in each situation.

1. You thought the movie started at 7:30, but when you walk into the theater, you see it has already started. You can't see your friends anywhere because it is really dark. What would you do? **Response:** I would wait until my eyes got used to the dark, then walk up and down the aisle and see if I could see them, or if they could see me.

2. You see an old friend of yours from school and say hello, but your friend looks at you and doesn't seem to recognize you. What would you do? **Response:** I would feel kind of embarrassed, but since I said hello to him, I guess I would tell him who I am and see if he remembers me.

3. Your boss at work gave you an important task to do, but you forgot what it was. You know it must be done before the end of the day, and your boss is in important meetings all day. What would you do? **Response:** It would be very hard to do, but I would go to my boss after one of his meetings and ask him what I was supposed to do. I would also apologize for forgetting and having to ask.

4. You are playing games in your yard when suddenly the ball accidentally goes through your neighbor's window. What would you do? **Response:** I would go over there and apologize to them and offer to pay to replace the window.

5. You are eating in a very nice restaurant and you accidentally spill your soup all over the table and yourself. Nobody in the restaurant notices. What would you do? **Response:** I would quickly get a napkin and wipe up the mess before anyone sees it.

6. Some people sitting next to you are talking in the library. Someone comes over and tells all of you to be quiet. You were not the one talking. What would you do? **Response:** I wouldn't do anything because I would want them to be quiet, too.

Vocabulary Match Work with a partner. Match the vocabulary words with the correct definition.

emperor	the ruler of an empire (larger than a kingdom)
strangers	people who nobody knows
invisible	not able to be seen
material	cloth used to make clothing
servant	someone who is hired to help or serve another person
parade	march up and down the street for people to see
fasten	to attach or make something tight, like a belt

Listen: The Schwa sound (1:8) Underline all of the schwa sounds that you hear.

1. He decid**ed** not **to** come for **a**nother hour.
2. I put the ob**j**ect in my pock**et**.
3. It will take **a**bout **an** hour.
4. She is **a** wonderful neigh**bor**.
5. The ma**ga**zine **con**tains pic**tures**.
6. The wom**en** talked **to**day.

Lesson 3

Listen: Vocabulary Fill-in (1:10) First, choose and write the correct word in the sentences below. Then listen to the speakers to check your answers.

1. The young woman's dress was **elegant** and expensive.
2. The older man **interrupted** the younger man as he was explaining.
3. His face and hands were **rough** looking and his clothes were torn and dirty.
4. There was **horror** in the woman's eyes when she saw that they were handcuffed.
5. The young man looked very **handsome** in his new suit.
6. The two men were **handcuffed** at the wrists.
7. The thief was caught by the **marshal** and sent to prison.
8. All of the passengers were sleeping in the **train car** except for the woman.

Listen: Practice (1:11) Listen to the situations. Place a number under the picture as it is being described.

1. Person A: "I want everyone to get down on the floor. If you do what I say nobody will get hurt. I want you two over there to start filling up this bag with money..."

2. Person A: "Hey, that's a great CD. Stand over there so that nobody can see me."
   Person B: "What are you doing? Put that back."
   Person A: "What's the big deal. It's only a CD."
   Person B: "Put it back. I don't want to be involved in shoplifting."

3. Person A: "Hey, stop that man. He stole my purse! Somebody stop him!"

4. Person A: "Did you see that guy? He almost caused an accident!" "He must have been in a hurry to run a red light like that."

5. Person A: "Sir, you were going 75 in a 55 mile an hour zone. I'm going to have to give you a ticket. Could I see your license and registration, please?
6. Person A: "But I didn't do anything!"
   Person B: "Selling drugs is a crime and you're going to jail. Watch your head as you get into the car."

Listen: The /i/ and /ee/ sounds (1:12) Circle the word that you hear the speaker say in the sentences below.
1. The old man (bit / **beat**) the dog with a stick.
2. He wants to buy a (**ship** / sheep).
3. The doctors said she is going to (**live** / leave).
4. Look at those pretty (chicks / **cheeks**).
5. He forgot to bring his (**mitt** / meat) to the party.

Lesson 4

Vocabulary Match Match the vocabulary word to its definition. Work in pairs or as a class.

fertile — rich with nutrients, usually referring to dirt or soil
sundown — time in which the sun goes down and night begins
miles — a measurement of 5,280 feet
barefoot — without shoes and/or socks
measure — to find the length by using some form of numbering
stumble — to trip and fall
urge — strong desire to do something

Listen: Practice (1:14) Listen to the speakers as they say an amount of money. Write out the amount.

1. $0.87
2. $2.48
3. $9.50
4. $16.35
5. $22.15
6. $56.28
7. $86.16
8. $135.86
9. $257.73
10. $500.55
11. $2,345.93
12. $4,218.35
13. $6,754.28
14. $12,237.85
15. $28,037.56

Listen: The /ae/ and /e/ sounds (1:15) Circle the word that you hear the speaker say in the sentences below.
1. This (**pan** / pen) is too small to use.
2. His friends (laughed / **left**) when he arrived.
3. Do you want to make a (bat / **bet**)?
4. Did you see the (**man** / men) over there?
5. Let's put the (axe / **X**) over there.

Lesson 5

Listen: Vocabulary Fill-in (1:17) First, choose and write the correct word in the sentences below. Then listen to the speakers to check your answers.
1. The people really liked the **community** a lot. They decided to stay.
2. The man was **obsessed** about getting sick. He wouldn't even leave the house.
3. He needed **proof** that the people were healthy before he would believe it.
4. The people **avoided** the young man because he looked really angry.
5. They decided to **permanently** stay in the small community.

Listen: Practice (1:18) Listen to each situation. Decide what the problem is with each person.
1. Brian: "I've tried everything, but I can't stop my nose from bleeding."
2. Sharon: "I just can't get out of bed this morning. I feel so weak that I can't do anything."
3. William: "I'm pretty sure that I just broke my arm."
4. Kathryn: "My tooth has been aching for days now. I think I need to see the dentist."
5. Cindy: "Wow, am I cold. I just can't seem to get warm."
6. Greg: "I need to see the doctor. I really cut my leg and it won't stop bleeding."
7. Robert: "I should make an appointment to see the doctor. I'm pretty sure I have an ear infection."

Listen: The /u/ and /oo/ sounds (1:19) Circle the word that you hear the speaker say in the sentences below.
1. He said that he was a little (**full** / fool).
2. The sign said (pull / **pool**) on the door.
3. I need to borrow ten (**bucks** / books) from you.
4. I think we'd better leave (son / **soon**).
5. (**Look** / Luke), the answer is simple if you'd listen to me.

Lesson 6

Vocabulary Match Match the vocabulary word to its definition. Work in pairs or as a class.

tame	not wild, a domesticated animal, or an animal that is friendly to humans
cave	an opening or hole inside a large rock or mountain
woods	another name for forest or group of trees
enemy	a person or group of people who are fighting against another person or group
bone	a hard structures of an animal's body, the framework of a body
guard	to protect from danger
grass	green plant that grows very short
hay	a plant that grows very long and is cut and fed to animals
servant	someone who serves another
wild	not tame, not being controlled or friendly to humans
pork	meat that comes from a pig
secretly	without anyone knowing, hidden, not easily seen

Listen: Practice (1:21) Listen to the following people describe the pets that they have. Write down the name of the animal(s) that each person has.

1. Jack: I have two pets. I have a dog named Rusty and a cat named Ruby. Amazingly enough, they actually get along great.
2. Karen: I have some goldfish in an aquarium. I guess you could call them pets.
3. Mike: Let's see, we have three dogs, two cats, and a parrot.
4. Sharon: My children raise rabbits as pets.

Listen: The /ae/ and /o/ sounds (1:22) Circle the word that you hear the speaker say in the sentences below.

1. The boy saw a (rack / **rock**) sitting outside the store.
2. The young girl received a (**pat** / pot) from her mother.
3. That's a pretty large (**bag** / bog).
4. He accidentally sat down on the (cat / **cot**).
5. The sign in the window said (**bat** / bought).

Lesson 7

Listen: Vocabulary Fill-in (2:2) First, choose and write the correct word in the sentences below. Then listen to the speakers to check your answers.

1. The cat **rubbed** itself against the baby's skin and it stopped crying.
2. The **grateful** woman began shaking hands and saying "thank you" to everyone.
3. The cat played with some **string** that was lying around on the floor.
4. The cat had a lot of **fur** that was warm and soft.
5. The cat **chased** the mouse all around the bedroom.
6. The boy was **pleased** with his progress in the class.
7. The woman **complimented** the small boy on how well he played the violin.
8. The dog tried to **bite** the man on the leg.
9. The student was very **clever** and got good grades in all her classes.
10. The woman was looking for a good **bargain** on clothes in the store.

Listen: Practice (2:3) Where is the cat? Listen to the speakers as they describe where the cat is. Write down the number next to the appropriate picture.

1. I can see a cat. It is sitting far away from the cave. (bottom-right)
2. The cat that I see is sitting on top of a large rock. (bottom-left)
3. I can see a cat sitting inside a cave. (top-middle)
4. The cat is sitting outside the cave. (top-left)
5. I can see a cat over there. It is sitting underneath that tree. (bottom-middle)
6. The cat is sitting next to the fire. (top-right)

Listen: The /or/ and /er/ sounds (2:4) Circle the word that you hear the speaker say in the sentences below.

1. Her mother told her she should (store / **stir**) the soup.
2. They went to the mall to buy some (**shorts** / shirts).
3. I think you have the wrong (**ward** / word).
4. She said that she wanted (four / **fur**).
5. He told us that it was a nice (form / **firm**).

Lesson 8

Vocabulary Match Match the vocabulary word to its definition. Work in pairs or as a class.

toboggan	a kind of sled for going down snowy hills
steep	nearly straight up or straight down (as a hill)

terror	extreme fright
whistled	a high sound, or a sound made by blowing
casually	not strict or formal, very loose and easy
march	to walk with a purpose, or to walk together in step
sailing	moving along easily and quickly (usually in a boat)
puzzled	not able to understand, confused
expression	an emotion or look on one's face
trick	a joke played on someone to fool them

Listen: Practice (2:6) Listen to the speakers. Write down the name of the person next to the activity that he/she loves to do.

1. Whenever I have some free time after work, I like to play basketball with some of my friends at the park.
2. I really like winter, especially when it snows a lot. I go skiing almost every weekend.
3. My roommates and I enjoy going dancing on Friday nights. Sometimes we go dancing on Saturday nights, too.
4. I like to have my friends come over, pop some popcorn, and watch movies at night.
5. My husband and I really like to socialize by going to restaurants. Sometimes we go out with friends, and sometimes alone.
6. My family loves spending time at the beach. Whenever I get vacation time, we always go to the beach.

Listen: The /ar/ and /er/ sounds (2:7) Circle the word that you hear the speaker say in the sentences below.

1. I don't think it is (**far** / fur).
2. She didn't think her speech was (hard / **heard**).
3. The children were looking at the (**cards** / curds).
4. He was looking for the (barn / **burn**) in the picture.
5. The doctor was worried about the girl's (**heart** / hurt) muscles.

Lesson 9

Listen: Vocabulary Fill-in (2:9) First, choose and write the correct word in the sentences below. Then listen to the speakers to check your answers.

1. The man had to wear a **wig** because he was losing his hair.
2. There were many different kinds of **brushes** on the counter to style her hair.
3. She looked at herself in the **mirror** as she was combing her hair.
4. The little boy counted fifteen **pennies** in his glass jar.
5. They didn't have very many **possessions** in their house.
6. The woman took the **lid** off the bottle and poured out the juice.
7. There were many different kinds of **combs** on the table at the beauty salon.

Listen: The /u/ and /er/ sounds (2:10) Circle the word that you hear the speaker say in the sentences below.

1. The big tree was covered with (**buds** / birds).
2. Look at all the (gulls / **girls**) on the beach.
3. They were looking for a little (**fun** / fern).
4. The people were looking at the (buns / **burns**).
5. The little boy saw the (cub / **curb**) from the tour bus.

Lesson 10

Listen: Practice (2:12) Listen to the speaker. Fill in the blanks with the words you hear.

Ernest never forgot the **story** about the Great Stone Face. He grew to become a hard-working, **intelligent** young man. Ernest **looked** at The Great Stone Face every day after finishing his **work**. He began to imagine that the **mountain** was his friend. He hoped for the day when he could meet the great **man** who resembled the mountain. He knew that he would **love** the man dearly.

Vocabulary Match Match the vocabulary word to its definition. Work in pairs or as a class.

respectable	being honored and admired by others
prophecy	a prediction of something to happen in the future
valley	a low area surrounded by hills and mountains
luxurious	very rich and good quality
gaze	to stare or to look at
resemble	to look like or to be similar in some way
rumor	a story that is passed on from one person to another
soldier	a person who fights in battles of war
industrious	working very hard

Listen: The /t/ and /d/ sounds (2:13) Circle the word that you hear the speaker say in the sentences below.

1. Do you want to (try / **dry**) this shirt?
2. The people were looking at the problems with the (**train** / drain).
3. He was looking at the (cart / **card**).
4. Jeremy was a (**bat** / bad) boy this summer.
5. Do you want to (write / **ride**) with the rest of us?

Lesson 11

Listen: Vocabulary Fill-in (2:15) First, choose and write the correct word in the sentences below. Then listen to the speakers to check your answers.

1. The famous **politician** gave a good speech to the people.
2. The man was **sincerely** concerned about the happiness of the people.
3. The **poet** gave some interesting stories about love and respect.
4. The two men sat down on a **bench** and talked for a while.
5. The boy was the most **popular** person in his whole class.
6. The man's **fame** was known throughout the whole community.
7. The news about the woman **spread** throughout the neighborhood.

Listen (11.3) The /l/ and /r/ sounds (2:16) Circle the word that you hear the speaker say in the sentences below.

1. The (pilot / **pirate**) was in charge of the other men.
2. She taught us how to (**play** / pray).
3. Please put this on your (list / **wrist**).
4. Don't step on the (**glass** / grass).
5. The answer was (long / **wrong**).

Lesson 12

Vocabulary Match Match the vocabulary word to its definition. Work in pairs or as a class.

soldier	a person who fights in a war
rifle	a long and thin gun
post	a place where a soldier stays and guards an area
duty	to perform a responsibility correctly; requirement
traitor	someone who rebels or fights against his/her own people
uniform	a special kind of clothing worn to identify people belonging to a special group
figure	form; shape
target	something to aim at (with a gun, perhaps)
firing	shooting a gun
company	a large group of soldiers in war
sergeant	a soldier who is in charge of other soldiers

Listen: Practice (2:18) Listen. Fill in the blanks below with the person describing himself/herself.

1. My name is John, and I write stories. Some of my stories are very famous.
2. My name is Sarah and I am the president of a large company in the United States.
3. I'm Roger and I teach high school math classes.
4. My name is Linda and I make movies in Hollywood.
5. I'm Brian and I play basketball professionally.
6. My name is Charles and I farm potatoes in Idaho.

Listen: The /ch/ and /sh/ sounds (2:19) Circle the word that you hear the speaker say in the sentences below.

1. I think I see some (**chips** / ships).
2. The people wanted to (catch / **cash**) some money.
3. He fell and hurt his (**chin** / shin).
4. She is (watching / **washing**) her car.
5. It was a story about three (**witches** / wishes).

Lesson 13

Listen: Vocabulary Fill-in (3:2) First, choose and write the correct word in the sentences below. Then listen to the speakers to check your answers.

1. She **insisted** on helping her mother clean the house.
2. The girl was taken to the ball in a large **carriage**.
3. The man was very **proud** of the fact that he won the game.
4. She had to **sew** up the clothes that had torn.
5. He wanted to **iron** his shirt because it was badly wrinkled.
6. The **mean** stepsisters did not help her do the work.

Listen: The /s/ and /sh/ sounds (3:3) Circle the word that you hear the speaker say in the sentences below.

1. Do you have a (**seat** / sheet) for me?
2. He didn't (save / **shave**) it yet.
3. They took a (sip / **ship**) from the water.
4. It is a big (**sock** / shock).
5. The people were all (**massed** / mashed) together.

Lesson 14

Listen: Practice (3:5) Listen to the speakers as they spell their names. Write them below.

1. D-A-V-I-D
2. S-U-S-A-N
3. J-A-S-O-N
4. K-I-M-B-E-R-L-Y
5. C-A-R-L-O-S
6. J-E-N-N-I-F-E-R
7. S-C-O-T-T-Y
8. K-E-L-L-Y
9. M-E-L-A-N-I-E
10. J-O-N-A-T-H-A-N

Vocabulary Match Match the vocabulary word to its definition. Work in pairs or as a class.

ache	have very sore and stiff muscles
candle	a long stick of wax with a wick inside, for burning to make light
quarry	a place where rocks are cut from the ground
fairy tales	stories about magic and princes and rescues
castle	beautiful palace or home where a king and queen live
rescue	save someone who is in danger
misery	long-time suffering
heart-broken	to have one's hopes destroyed suddenly
postman	a person who delivers the mail
robbers	people who steal money or things from others
mules	animals, like horses or donkeys, used to carry heavy objects

Listen: The /s/ and /th/ sounds (3:6) Circle the word that you hear the speaker say in the sentences below.

1. It looks a little (sick / **thick**).
2. They were looking for the (**pass** / path).
3. It's just a little (sin / **thin**).
4. The young man doesn't want to (**sink** / think).
5. It's a really big (sum / **thumb**).

Lesson 15

Listen: Practice (3:8) Listen to the speakers. Write down what each person is afraid of.

1. Steven: I've always been afraid of snakes. I hate snakes.
2. Julie: I'm really scared of walking alone at night. I get so afraid when I'm walking alone on a dark night.
3. Kevin: I'm afraid of heights. When I'm up high looking down, I get really nervous.
4. Susan: I'm afraid of water, like in a swimming pool. I don't know why, but I'm afraid of the water.
5. Chad: I'm afraid of flying in an airplane. I fly quite a lot, but I still get scared of airplanes.
6. Rebecca: I'm afraid of spiders inside the house. When I see a spider, I have my husband get rid of it.
7. John: I've always been afraid of having to fight in a war. War really scares me.
8. Cindy: I'm afraid that my kids will have a car accident. Both my kids drive cars and it scares me to death.
9. George: I'm afraid of dogs. I don't know why, but as a child I hated dogs and I still get nervous around them.
10. Barbara: I'm afraid of losing my job. Without my job, I don't know how I'd find another one.

Listen: Vocabulary Fill-in (3:9) First, choose and write the correct word in the sentences below. Then listen to the speakers to check your answers.

1. The people wanted to get **rid** of the Griffin from their community.
2. The Griffin was an **awful** creature to look at.
3. Because he was tired, he decided to take a short **nap**.
4. The man could see his **reflection** in the mirror.
5. The young **priest** was asked to take the Griffin out of the town.
6. The statue was **carved** out of a large piece of rock.

Listen: The /s/ and /z/ sounds (3:10) Circle the word that you hear the speaker say in the sentences below.

1. I have never seen (**ice** / eyes) like that before.
2. The (prices / **prizes**) looked very expensive.
3. Can you hear the (**bus** / buzz)?
4. Those (once / **ones**) looked very nice.
5. I am looking for (**Miss** / Ms.) Taylor.

Lesson 16

Listen: Practice (3:12) Listen. Match the speakers to the changes they would like to make in life.

1. Stephanie   "I would like to spend more time with my family, especially on weekends."
2. James   "I want to exercise more often. I'm really out of shape."
3. Barbara   "I think I should learn how to swim. I'm almost 30 years old and I still don't know how."
4. Greg   "I want to change my job to something more challenging."
5. Wendy   "I would like to spend more time reading. I used to read all the time."
6. David   "I need to learn how to cook better meals. I eat too much fast food."
7. Kathy   "I want to work less in the office and go out more often with my friends, especially on weekends."

Vocabulary Match Match the vocabulary word to its definition. Work in pairs or as a class.

wilderness   the forest, or desert that is far away from the city and people
routine   an action that is done over and over again
repulsive   something disgusting; sickening
appetite   hunger
feasta big meal with very special food
cowards   people who are afraid; not brave
selfish   wanting only to satisfy oneself, thinking only of oneself
cruel   mean, unkind
herbs   plants that can be used to heal, or to eat
threat   promising punishment if something is not done

Listen: The /d/ and /the/ sounds (3:13) Circle the word that you hear the speaker say in the sentences below.

1. (Day / **They**) came at about 7:00 a.m.
2. I don't want (D's / **these**) for my grades.
3. (**Dave** / they've) already brought some food.
4. Are you making (**dares** / theirs)?
5. Are those animals in the zoo (breeding / **breathing**)?

Lesson 17

Listen: Practice (3:15) Listen to the situations. Circle how the speaker is feeling."

Person 1:   "I am so upset at her right now. She really made me **angry** with the things she said about me."
Person 2:   "I don't like being out here so late at night all by ourselves. This place is **scaring** me. Let's go back home."
Person 3:   "I'm really glad (**happy**) that you invited me to the party. I'm having a great time. You really made my day."
Person 4:   "I can't believe that I spilled red punch all over her dress. I'm so **embarrassed**. I should just leave."
Person 5:   "My grandmother passed away last week. I'm still feeling **sad** because she and I were really close."
Person 6:   "I have to sing in front of the whole school tonight and I'm really **nervous**. I hope I do okay and don't make mistakes."
Person 7:   "This test is impossible! I'll never get it done in time. I'm so **frustrated** with this biology class!"
Person 8:   "Your new car is so nice! I wish I had a car like that. I'm so **jealous** of you right now!

Listen: The /ch/ and /j/ sounds (3:16) Circle the word that you hear the speaker say in the sentences below.

1. The crowd was (**cheering** / jeering) when the team scored.
2. I think those are (chains / **Jane's**), aren't they?
3. You forgot your (H / **age**) on this application.
4. I thought that the man was (**choking** / joking).
5. Those are (**cherries** / Jerry's), I think.

Lesson 18

Listen: Practice (3:18) Listen to the weather forecast. Fill in the blanks with the words you hear.

Today we should see mostly **cloudy** skies. Lights **winds** are forecast for this afternoon. The high for today is expected to be around **55** degrees. The low for tonight should be around **32** degrees. Tomorrow there is a **50%** chance of **rain** in the afternoon and a chance of **snow** in the mountains. Scattered rain **showers** are likely tomorrow night, with snow falling in the **mountains**. Highs tomorrow should be in the upper **40s** and lows should be in the lower **20s**. Currently we have a temperature of **42** degrees under mostly **cloudy** skies.

Listen: Vocabulary Fill-in (3:19) First, choose and write the correct word in the sentences below. Then listen to the speakers to check your answers.

1. Because of the extreme cold, the man's fingers were **numb** and he couldn't feel them.
2. The people were **unfamiliar** with the city and didn't know where they were going.
3. The two men went fishing at a small **creek** in the mountains.
4. She **lit** a match to start the fire.
5. The people were **shocked** when they heard the news.
6. The man **rubbed** his hands together to try to get them warm.

Listen: The /k/ and /g/ sounds (3:20) Circle the word that you hear the speaker say in the sentences below.

1. She has a lot of (**cuts** / guts), doesn't she?
2. This is a large (class / **glass**), isn't it?
3. That is a very large (**coat** / goat).
4. The (clue / **glue**) is sitting right over there.
5. It looks like it may be (**cold** / gold).

Lesson 19

Listen: Practice (4:2) Listen to the speakers. Write down what makes each person go crazy (upset).

1. Lewis "My roommate always plays country music really loud in his room. It drives me crazy sometimes."
2. Rachel "My husband drives too fast. It makes me nervous the way he drives."
3. Dean "My friend always shows up 15 minutes late for everything. It makes me go nuts always waiting for him."
4. Angela "My husband snores when he sleeps. Sometimes the snoring really bothers me at night."
5. Mark "There is this stupid commercial that always comes on television during my favorite program. It drives me nuts."
6. Lisa "I get the house completely clean and then my kids mess it all up. It makes me so mad when they do that."

Vocabulary Match Match the vocabulary word to its definition. Work in pairs or as a class.

clever	smart, intelligent
revenge	wanting to punish another for what he/she did to you
ray	a small line of light
spying	secretly watching
groan	a low sound made when someone is afraid or in pain
lantern	an object that will carry a flame inside for light
obsessed	thinking about something all the time
beat	to hit
rid (of)	to make something leave or be gone

Listen: The /w/ and /v/ sounds (4:3) Circle the word that you hear the speaker say in the sentences below.

1. I have never seen a (**whale** / veil) like that.
2. That (wheel / **veal**) doesn't look very good.
3. The (**West** / vest) is very pretty.
4. The (wines / **vines**) are in good condition.
5. Her message is a little (**worse** / verse).

Lesson 20

Listen: Practice (4:5) Listen to the speaker. Fill in the clocks with the times you hear.

1. The time right now is a quarter after seven.
2. The time is twenty-five minutes to three.
3. The time right now is ten minutes after nine.
4. The time right now is five minutes to midnight.
5. The time is six forty.
6. The time is a quarter to five.

Listen: Vocabulary Fill-in (4:6) First, choose and write the correct word in the sentences below. Then listen to the speakers to check your answers.

1. The men picked up their **weapons** and prepared for the battle.
2. Many people want to improve their bodies by exercising their **muscles**.
3. Babies learn to **crawl** before they can walk.
4. The people wanted to take a hike through the beautiful **forest**.
5. The people found some old **bones** buried in the sand.
6. The man followed the **trail** out of the jungle.

Lesson 21

Listen: Practice (4:9) Listen. Write down what each person is studying in college.

1. Tom — "Right now I'm studying biology. I want to become a high school biology teacher."
2. Terry — "My major in college is history."
3. Holly — "I'm studying math. I want to become a math professor some day."
4. Wayne — "I'm majoring in computer science. I enjoy working with computers."
5. Sally — "My major is English literature."
6. Jamie — "I'm studying business. I want to get my Master's degree in business administration.
7. Greg — "My major is in chemistry."
8. Nicole — "I'm majoring in fine arts. Fine arts includes art, dance, and theater."
9. Brian — "I'm studying to become a nurse."
10. Amanda — "Right now I'm taking general education classes. I don't have a major, yet."

Vocabulary Match Match the vocabulary word to its definition. Work in pairs or as a class.

landlady	a person who manages an apartment or house
pipe	an object that can be used for smoking tobacco
match	a small piece of wood or cardboard hit against a rough surface which makes fire
attorney	someone who understands the law and works for others; lawyer
shrink	to become smaller or less significant
respected	well-liked by others, admired
railing	metal pieces or wood used for support on stairs; fence
lots	pieces of land
model	someone that others wish to follow or be like

Listen: Word Endings (4:10) Listen to the speakers say the following words. Repeat after the speakers. Circle the ending that is used.

-es ending				**-ed ending**			
apples	/s/	**/z/**	/uz/	grabbed	**/d/**	/t/	/ud/
loses	/s/	/z/	**/uz/**	cracked	/d/	**/t/**	/ud/
boxes	/s/	/z/	**/uz/**	hurried	**/d/**	/t/	/ud/
tents	**/s/**	/z/	/uz/	laughed	/d/	**/t/**	/ud/
maps	**/s/**	/z/	/uz/	spied	**/d/**	/t/	/ud/
pens	/s/	**/z/**	/uz/	smacked	/d/	**/t/**	/ud/
pies	/s/	**/z/**	/uz/	hunted	/d/	/t/	**/ud/**
laughs	**/s/**	/z/	/uz/	mopped	/d/	**/t/**	/ud/

Listen to the speakers say the following sentences. Circle the word you hear.

1. My friend (**can** / can't) go with us.
2. I (can / **can't**) drive a truck.
3. She (**can** / can't) speak Japanese.
4. (Can / **Can't**) you help me?
5. She (**can** / can't) talk right now.
6. The secretary (can / **can't**) help you.
7. My brother (can / **can't**) sing very well.
8. We (**can** / can't) go to the movie tonight.
9. I (can / **can't**) come tonight.
10. (**Can** / Can't) you come?
11. He (**can** / can't) play the violin.
12. (Can / **Can't**) you dance very well?
13. We (**can** / can't) study here right now.
14. Our baby (can / **can't**) talk.
15. I (can / **can't**) see it from here.

Lesson 22

Listen: Practice (4:12) Listen. Circle if the person's experience was lucky or unlucky.

1. Peter: "I went to Las Vegas a few weeks ago and lost over $500." (**Unlucky**)
2. David: "I was walking to school when I found a five dollar bill just lying on the sidewalk." (**Lucky**)
3. Sarah: "I went skiing last weekend and fell down and broke my leg." (**Unlucky**)
4. Katy: "I didn't study very hard for my math test, but I still got a 97 percent on it." (**Lucky**)
5. Nathan: "I didn't think that Linda would go out with me Friday night, but I asked her and I couldn't believe she said yes." (**Lucky**)
6. Rachel: "We played as hard as we could during the soccer game, but the other team scored a goal in the last 10 seconds and won the game." (**Unlucky**)
7. Brent: "I was in the locker room taking a shower after playing basketball. When I returned to my locker, someone had stolen my new shoes." (**Unlucky**)
8. Paula: "I wasn't feeling very well, so I went to the doctor. She said that I have the flu." (**Unlucky**)
9. Daniel: "I thought that because of the weather, I'd have to cancel the picnic I had planned with my girlfriend. But it turned out to be a warm and sunny day, so we were able to go." (**Lucky**)
10. Amy: "I just got a letter from the university I applied to. They accepted me and offered me a scholarship." (**Lucky**)

Listen: Vocabulary Fill-in (4:13) First, choose and write the correct word in the sentences below. Then listen to the speakers to check your answers.

1. The person who had died was placed in a wooden **coffin**.
2. The man .**claimed** the box to be his.
3. The people stood on the **platform** waiting for the train.
4. The smell was **intolerable** and the people walked out of the room.
5. There was a terrible **stench** that came from the old house.
6. The two men breathed in the bad-smelling air with their **nostrils**.

Let's Talk: Lucky Guess Answers to the riddles on page 97.

Riddle #1: A quarter and a nickel. (One is not a quarter.)
Riddle #2: The parrot was deaf.
Riddle #3: I am referring to myself.
Riddle #4: Nowhere. Survivors are not buried because they are still alive.
Riddle #5: A grandmother, a mother, and a daughter. (Three people. Both women have daughters.)
Riddle #6: Both are the same distance because they are together at the same point.
Riddle #7: They are two members of triplets.
Riddle #8: The same number (20) as before. The ship stays on top of the water, so the ladder is not affected.
Riddle #9: 27 days. On the 27th day the spider crawls up 4 meters and escapes from the hole.
Riddle #10: The second doctor is the boy's mother.

Listen: Word Stress (4:14) Listen to the following words. They have been divided into syllables. Put a stress mark (') above the syllable that you hear being stressed. The first one has been done for you.

yes' ter day	a no' ther	chil' dren	ba na' na	a gain'
for get'	help' ful	com' pa ny	va ca' tion	tel' e phone

Lesson 23

Listen: Practice (4:16) Listen. Write down what each person's future plans are.

1. I plan to go to college in about a year from now.
2. I think that I'll travel around Europe for a little while.
3. I plan on getting married and having a family.
4. In the future I will probably get a job and work.
5. My future plans are to learn English and then become a translator.
6. I want to move to Hawaii and get a job there.
7. I plan on going to graduate school and becoming a doctor.
8. I'm not sure what I'll do in the future. I haven't really thought about it.
9. One of my future plans includes traveling around the United States.
10. I'd like to learn another language in the future.

Vocabulary Match Match the vocabulary word to its definition. Work in pairs or as a class.

cellar	a place underneath the house; similar to basement
barn	a place where animals and farming equipment are kept
hay	similar to grass; used as food for animals
stove	an appliance used to cook food
furniture	couch, chairs, sofa, table, etc.
gasp	to show shock or fear; breathe in hard from surprise
leaned	rested on something: bent downward
weep(ing)	crying; showing sadness